Pensioned off

RETHINKING AGEING SERIES

Series editor: Brian Gearing
                School of Health and Social Welfare
                The Open University

The rapid growth in ageing populations in Britain and other countries has led to a dramatic increase in academic and professional interest in the subject. Over the past decade this has led to the publication of many research studies which have stimulated new ideas and fresh approaches to understanding old age. At the same time, there has been concern about continued neglect of ageing and old age in the education and professional training of most workers in health and social services, and about inadequate dissemination of the new information and ideas about ageing to a wider public.

This series aims to fill a gap in the market for accessible, up-to-date studies of important issues in ageing. Each book will focus on a topic of current concern addressing two fundamental questions: what is known about this topic? And what are the policy, service and practice implications of our knowledge? Authors will be encouraged to develop their own ideas, drawing on case material, and their own research, professional or personal experience. The books will be interdisciplinary, and written in clear, non-technical language which will appeal to a broad range of students, academics and professionals with a common interest in ageing and age care.

Current and forthcoming titles:
Simon Biggs *et al.*: **Elder abuse in perspective**
Ken Blakemore and Margaret Boneham: **Age, race and ethnicity:
     A comparative approach**
Joanna Bornat (ed.): **Reminiscence reviewed: Perspectives,
     evaluations, achievements**
Joanna Bornat and Maureen Cooper: **Older learners**
Bill Bytheway: **Ageism**
Beverley Hughes: **Older people and community care: Critical theory
     and practice**
Anne Jamieson: **Comparing policies of care for older people**
Eric Midwinter: **Pensioned off: Retirement and income examined**
Sheila Peace *et al.*: **Re-evaluating residential care**
Moyra Sidell: **Health in old age: Myth, mystery and management**
Andrew Sixsmith: **Quality of life: Rethinking well-being in old age**
Robert Slater: **The psychology of growing old**
Alan Walker and Tony Maltby: **Ageing Europe**

Pensioned off
Retirement and income examined

ERIC MIDWINTER

OPEN UNIVERSITY PRESS
Buckingham · Philadelphia

Open University Press
Celtic Court
22 Ballmoor
Buckingham
MK18 1XW

and
1900 Frost Road, Suite 101
Bristol, PA 19007, USA

First Published 1997

A catalogue record of this book is available from the British Library

ISBN 0 335 19682 9 (pbk)   0 335 19683 7 (hbk)

Library of Congress Cataloging-in-Publication Data

Midwinter, Eric C.
    Pensioned off : retirement and income examined / Eric Midwinter.
        p.   cm. — (Rethinking ageing)
    Includes bibliographical references and index.
    ISBN 0-335-19683-7 (hbk)   ISBN 0-335-19682-9 (pbk)
    1. Old age pensions—Great Britain.   2. Retirement—Great Britain.   I. Title.   II.
Series: Rethinking ageing series.
    HD7106.35.G7M53   1997
    331.25'2'0941—dc21   96-39961
                                                                              CIP

Typeset by Type Study, Scarborough
Printed in Great Britain by Biddles Limited, Guildford and Kings Lynn

Contents

List of tables

Series editor's preface

The aim of the 'Rethinking Ageing' series has been to present what is currently known about important contemporary topics in gerontology in a way which is informative, thought-provoking and accessible to a wide range of people involved in work with older people including practitioners and researchers. So far the series has included books on race and ethnicity; reminiscence; ageism; the psychology of growing old; health in old age; elder abuse; ageing in Europe; and residential care. This is a wide range of topics, all of them of contemporary interest and relevance. With the publication of *Pensioned off: Retirement and income examined* by Eric Midwinter we are able to add a vital issue of contemporary policy to those covered so far.

Retirement affects some twelve million people, nearly a quarter of the population, and fifty years after the Beveridge reforms which were thought to have solved the problem, poverty remains an acute issue in old age. Moreover, economic inequality characterizes older age: not only is income in old age distributed unequally, that inequality starts much earlier in the life cycle, a major determinant being the way old age income is generated differentially between different groups according to their patterns of work over a lifetime. As *Pensioned off* makes clear, work, retirement, and the State's provision of a pension according to age criteria, are fundamental to our understanding of the social experience of ageing in modern society. Furthermore, the allocation of national expenditure to income in retirement is a crucial determinant of quality of life in old age.

This is the first book in the 'Rethinking Ageing' series to give a significant historical overview of the development of policy. Eric Midwinter's analysis reveals the way in which, historically, the subject of retirement has been intertwined with the social definition of the older person and old age. It is the fact of retirement from paid work, and the reaching of the pension age, which more than anything else marks out in public perception what it is to be old. For work (and the pressure to ration or reduce it), itself a consequence of industrial technology, has been the driving force in the implementation of retirement processes. Indeed, Midwinter suggests that 'retirement' is extremely new in historical time, a hundred years old at most, and work remains central to the whole pattern of income maintainance in old age.

This book is divided into three parts: respectively, past, present and future. In Part I, 'Past imperfect', Eric Midwinter shows that cultural perception – the images of old age and older people – is crucial to the provision of pensions and other welfare services in later life. This has been true historically and remains the case today. The treatment of older people in society both past and present is characterized by a deep-rooted ambivalence which has affected the atmosphere in which the political debate has occurred in both the nineteenth and twentieth centuries and in both funding and services. This cultural ambivalence makes fundamental reforms very difficult to achieve for fundamental change has to address the ageism of society as well as economic inequality throughout society. Part I also contains much fascinating incidental historical detail. How many of us know for example that the first public retirement pension was paid in 1684 to Martin Horsham, a land waiter of the Port of London? Or that it was not until the nineteenth century that the two terms 'retirement' and 'pension' became popular parlance?

The second part of the book focuses on the present day position and combines detailed analysis of older people's incomes with an examination of the cultural context in which retirement occurs. One of the book's strengths is the way it integrates the specific analysis of statistical information into the broad policy sweep, dealing adroitly with demographic data, income and expenditure as they affect retirement today.

The final part presents an interesting division into the 'likely' and the 'ideal' future. Because fundamental reform is so difficult to achieve the author divides his prognosis in two: first, he considers what is likely to happen given the current cultural and political parameters; and, second, he proffers his ideal solution.

Eric Midwinter is a man of many parts: educationalist, historian, policy analyst, and a highly respected gerontologist who was formerly Director of the Centre of Policy on Ageing. He is therefore very well qualified to write a book on income and retirement. His book is also extremely topical at the present time when pensions and how to pay for them are a matter of heated debate between the political parties. The 'demographic time bomb' and other alarmist scenarios are familiar from our newspapers and ambivalence to older people remains a chief underlying characteristic. This book brings a much needed historical perspective and a lucid and eloquent analysis to the contemporary debate.

Brian Gearing
School of Health and Social Welfare
The Open University

Introduction

It is very important to recognize that it is not chronological age but status which determines the history and current reality of older age. It is, in a simple phrase, not age but stage that matters. If older people contrived to live a similar life to younger people, the issue would be much less significant. If they continued to work and raise families, if, in other words, they maintained the normal day by day activities of other adults, there would scarcely be a question raised. Indeed where older people do pursue paid work, perhaps as politicians or artists, and family rearing, perhaps with a second family, into older age, they do not warrant a different 'old age' viewpoint.

The fact is that, in modern times, the status of the majority of older people has altered radically. They have ceased work, frequently at an age much earlier than in eras gone by, and their children have reached years of independence often, again, with their parents at a younger age than in generations past. This is a new phenomenon, at least on a large scale. Throughout history, and across geography, in all human societies, very few have reached the point of yielding up work and completing childrearing tasks. Now it is the norm for people to finish paid work and parenting at a much earlier age; in fact, in many societies it was normal, and in some it still is, for them to work until they were decrepit or dead. Additionally, many people now have smaller families (although larger families are not unknown in some parts of the world) and thus the parenting phase is completed more quickly.

This has created the novel idea of 'retirement', a period after paid work and parenthood, and, importantly, now a relatively long period. It is a new development, at least in terms of ordinary existence. In the United Kingdom it is barely 100 years old, a mere flick of the eyelid when one recalls that agricultural settlement and stable domestic life has been a feature of these islands for as long as 2500 years.

Of course, the number of people involved is meaningful. The survival rates of the British, as of all developed nations, means that the bulk of the population is practically guaranteed a period of life beyond their sixtieth birthday. Currently, some 11 or 12 million people over 60, out of a population of some 58 million in the United Kingdom, have finished work and/or completed their parenting duties. It is a huge proportion of the population, but, clearly, in previous generations, many would have remained at work and many would have found themselves still acting out the roles of mother or father. Indeed, a considerable section of that retired population today are under 60 years of age.

Perhaps the simplest way to describe the phenomenon is to mark the coupling of two strong determinants: early release from work with later death. It is these two factors which have opened up this massive new category of person, who, with their actual age ranging from the early 50s to over 100, are in the stage of non-work and non-childcare obligation. Hitherto, the social and economic rule of thumb had been straightforward. People worked to keep themselves and their dependent children, and that was that. Heaven knows it was a hit and miss business, with famine, poverty and starvation frequently the lot of ordinary people, but that was the social construct. In relative terms, those too old to work and without recourse to some extended family support had always been so few in number, and had survived in that condition for such a short period, that they were never more than a blip on the temperature chart of social and political policy. Many found, indeed many find, succour from their grown children or other family members so that overall, before the industrial era, the social problem of old people *en masse* was rarely thrust to the top of the governmental agenda.

Over the last 100 or so years, in the United Kingdom as in other developed nations, that situation has changed rapidly and vividly. The question of how to procure a sufficiency of funding and allied supports in kind for this numerous cohort became pressing during the nineteenth, and has become substantially more pressing during the twentieth century. At its simplest, and there is no novelty about this, there are two solutions – either private or public provision. People rely, then, either on their own resources, typically now through an occupational pension, with perhaps some dependence on investment or the support of their family, or on state pension and other benefits. Naturally, a large proportion enjoys a mix of the two brands, and needless to say the two styles are not completely separate; public tax policy may assist private pension arrangements, and people have usually paid taxes or national insurance payments out of their private incomes as contributions to the state benefits.

In addition, there is the matter of services, such as welfare and health assistance, and the part they play in determining an older person's quality of life. The basic question is a simple one: does the individual pay or does the state, through central or local government, provide? It is not, in practice, as simple as all that. For instance, the individual may be in receipt of public benefits or tax concessions which help as he or she buys in private services, while the state services – home helps, meals on wheels, for instance – may be offered not freely but at a price. By and large, however, the key to an understanding of both income maintenance and its concomitant health and other services is an awareness of that private/public balance, and it is that which dictates the format of this study. Policy decisions are not culture-free. The view of old age in any society very much determines how the public and the politicians resolve, for example, how generous or how stingy the level of pensions might be. Discussion of this social context has been included for without it core policy statements make little sense.

In an attempt to throw some light on these questions, the book is divided into three unequal parts. The first and middle-sized section traces the origins and compass of retirement in the United Kingdom and the steps taken to sustain it, especially in regard to income maintenance, but with some scrutiny of services in kind, and some consideration of the prevailing perception of older age. The second and largest section deals with the current manifestation of those issues – the numbers and characteristics of retired people, the way they are funded, how otherwise they are supported, and how old age is perceived. The third and shortest section finally looks ahead to the future apropos these same issues, and comments, optimistically, on what should be done and, pessimistically, on what will probably happen.

PART I

Past imperfect: Post-work people yesterday

1

The history of old age and retirement

Living longer or dying later?

'People are living longer nowadays.' First let us deal with that glib and misleading half-truth. Plainly, some people have always 'lived longer'. The maximum lifespan of the human species is about 115 years, and there have always been a few who have approached that formidable target. There is little evidence that humanity is seriously making biological inroads into that maximum figure; people, as a species, are certainly not living longer (Evans 1993). Between the Battle of Hastings in 1066 and the Battle of the Somme in 1916 there was always a substantial number of older people in Britain; we find, for instance, 'proportions aged 60 and above, at some 8% on average over the whole length of time known to us . . . in England' (Laslett 1989). There has always been older age.

How has this confusion arisen? What has happened is that the actuarial calculation about life expectancy has been widely misinterpreted. In a recent and excellent biography of Tom Paine (Keane 1995), the eighteenth-century political philosopher and activist, the author partially explains Tom Paine's teenage wanderlust by his 'sense that his life had passed the half-way mark (the average life-expectancy at the time was a mere 37 years)'. Life expectancy at birth in the 1750s was, it is true, 37 years. But, apart from the fact that a youthful staymaker's apprentice would scarcely have been aware of the statistic, this did not mean that hundreds fell from the twig when they were 37. It is an *average* life expectancy, considerably dragged down in this case by a fifth of the babies dying in infancy.

To take a slightly later example from the industrial era, of Lancashire's 102,025 deaths in 1841, 83,616 were under 20, and the average age of death was 22. In parts of Liverpool in the 1840s the average fell as low as 17 (Playfair 1845). This was largely because of the thousands who died before the age of 1 year. It did not mean that phalanxes of 22-year-old Lancastrians or 17-year-old Liverpudlians were keeling over in the fever-strewn streets.

Survival is the key. If, even in such parlous times, you could edge past your first birthday, and then, escaping childhood killer illnesses, your fifth birthday, and then, avoiding the rigours of childbirth, the horrific epidemics and fatal accidents of the workplace, your early adulthood, there was no reason why you might not struggle through to 60, and even set your ambitious sights on that far-off bourn of 115 years. An intriguing quiz question is to ask: what is the difference between life expectancy at 60 in 1900 and now? Many people quote a large differential. However, depending on whether one is male or female, the difference is only about four to six years. Granted, at 60, that is quite a bonus, but the point remains that, if one reached 60 in 1900, your chances of a few more years were quite strong. It is getting to 60 that counts.

The upshot is that, whereas only 6 to 10 per cent were managing that in the centuries before World World I (1914–18), the figure is now much closer to 20 per cent, to the juncture where there is a reasonable guarantee that most people will make the 60-year grade. It is not a matter of people living longer, but of people dying later, between which there is a significant difference. Throughout history, death has struck randomly across the age range; in point of fact, it may be more accurate to say that, far from being random, it has struck with harsh ferocity at babies. In 1900, out of a United Kingdom population of about 41 million, 156,000 people died before the age of 1. In 1990, out of a larger population of some 57 million, a lesser number – 128,000 – died before the age of 65. In 1900 the dangerous age was under 1. Nowadays the dangerous age is over 65. Only one death in seven occurs before the age of 65; the old have monopolized death, and a good thing, too.

Curiously, one of the causes of this amazing switch around in the incidence of death has been lowered birthrates. The birthrate was over 35 per 1000 of the population as late as the 1860s, and about 30 per 1000 a century ago; the birthrate today is 12 to 13. Since about the 1870s, the combined effects of hygiene and welfare, birth control and changed social attitudes (for instance, it became fashionable to have small families) has resulted in many fewer babies being born. The great majority of that smaller number survived, having been better cared for and cosseted, so that overall what might be called demographic productivity has been more efficient. In brief, reasonable fertility, allied with very much improved infant mortality, has ensured that generations of people would be available to survive into older age.

Moreover, that very reduction in the number of children born has also contributed to the perceived size of the 'old age' population, for it must be remembered that we are dealing with *proportions*. The proportion of older people in the United Kingdom is approximately 20 per cent, but one good reason for that is because the proportion of younger people has dropped to almost the same amount. During the twentieth century, the proportion of older people has risen from about 6 per cent to about 20 per cent, and the proportion of younger people has dropped from about 32 per cent to nearer 20 per cent. One amount has trebled, as the other has decreased by a third; the one is a function of the other.

In other words, the increase in the number of older people, so misleadingly described as 'people living longer', has much to do with the decrease in younger people, and the fact that, for the first time, there are now more old age pensioners than there are children on the school registers. In mid-Victorian Britain nearly half of the population was under 20, and less than a quarter was over 45, giving the population a median age of 24, and with nearly two-thirds of this youthful population unmarried (Read 1979). No wonder there was so much public concern about organized sports and youth movements, and rather less about the needs of the relatively few older people. By the end of the twentieth century the median age of the population will be just under 38, that is, half the population will be over and half under that age. Over the century the mean or average age has risen from 27 to over 37.

Try and visualize the pattern if the same younger proportion had been preserved, but had enjoyed the benefits of improved health and allied care. The consequence, of course, would have been a much larger population, probably in the region of 80 or 90 million. Thus the proportion of older people has not grown in real terms quite as much as we tend to think or as is often inferred, because of this huge downward shift in the number of younger people. In 1900 one in six *adults* (that is, over 16) was over 60; today the same ratio is one in four. That makes for an interesting feature and perhaps one that should figure more readily in social policy deliberations. If one thinks of the younger and older sections of the population as dependent and the middle or mainline adult section as working, one finds that the middle group has remained virtually unchanged as a proportion of the population at about 64 per cent. The sum of the two fractions, old and young, was about 36 per cent in 1900, and it is much the same now – it is just that the make-up of that total is entirely changed in character, from many to few young and few to many old people.

An ageing world

It is instructive to place this narrower account of old age in the United Kingdom in the global context. Population is, of course, the chief factor. At a conservative estimate, the human species has numbered between 60 and 80 billion since, some million or more years ago, our remotest ancestors first put in an appearance. Needless to say, a huge number of these died at an early age; it might not be too melodramatic to suggest that a majority would not have survived childhood. Around 10,000 BC, with humankind dependent upon food-gathering, including some hunting and fishing, our planet housed no more than five to 10 million people. About that time the cultivation of crops and the domestication of animals was the basis of the so-called agrarian revolution, and, by the end of the eighteenth century, with many regions devoted to agricultural habits, the world population had raced to between 650 and 850 million. By about the middle of the nineteenth century the earth's population reached one billion (Cipolla 1962).

Since then the figures have leapt astronomically. By the mid-twentieth century the population trebled to three billion, and it could well double again by the end of this century. By 2025 it is likely to have reached over eight billion, 10 times what it was in 1750. In pre-agrarian conditions, it is thought that very few survived beyond what we would now term middle age, and, although, as we have noted, older age was not a novelty in Britain's olden days, it was, worldwide, something of a rarity. Indeed, as late as the mid-1980s, the world percentage of over 65s was less than 6 per cent, and that proportion had not grown much since the first half of the century, despite the doubling of the global population. Interestingly, it was close to the British figure during the previous centuries.

By the end of the first quarter of the twenty-first century that position will have changed radically. Then there are likely to be 800 million people over 65, well over three times the number in the mid-1980s. They will constitute nearly 10 per cent of the world population, approaching a doubling of the current percentage. It may be observed that the developed nations have more or less completed their demographic transformations, and, in general, a similar process is occurring over the rest of the planet. For example, the proportion of the European population in 2025 who will be over 65 will be more than 18 per cent, nearly twice the world average. What cannot be gainsaid is the massive worldwide increase in older people; by the year 2000 there will be as many older people on earth as there were people of all ages 300 years ago in 1700 (United Nations 1986).

Attention should again be drawn to the youth element. The ascending proportion of older people is to some degree dictated by the descending proportion of younger people; the percentage of people under 14 years of age is destined to fall from a third, which it has been for most of this century, to a quarter by 2025. Where in 1950 children outnumbered old persons by seven to one, by 2025 it will be only five to two, a wholesale change in what from time immemorial has been an unaltered ratio.

The cause and effect relationship of population and economic activity is very complex. Is increased population the lever for improved economic effort and initiative, or does economic invention and productivity permit higher population? This is not the place to discuss the many aspects of that debate. Suffice it to mark the march, fast becoming a gallop, of world population, and the line of older age within that parade, and then to re-mark the economic environment through which the march processes.

The agriculturally based economy has often been self-sufficient, and might largely be defined as a 'natural economy', that is one in which people live mainly off their own produce and exchange is often in kind. A typical example might be medieval English manors, which numbered some 10,000 in the reign of Edward I in the thirteenth century. Each manor, normally supporting no more than a hundred or so souls, was chiefly devoted to subsistence agriculture, usually over quite wide areas and with normally poorish yields. The type of farming varied according to the conditions of the terrain and the soil, but there was frequently a 'fallow' tract left for recuperation. Equally, there was a wide variation in tenure, but the guiding principle was that pieces of land were let by the landowner – 'the lord of the manor' – to the families under his control in return for rents, often in kind, and duties such as military service and help with the landowner's personal farming. It has rarely been an exclusive practice, in that the use of money has a long-standing history, but the build-up of trading and commercial activity and the move to a more predominantly money economy only became prominent from about the sixteenth century onwards, at least in European terms. In turn, the industrial revolution, dating from about 1750 and first located in Britain, gave a decided emphasis to commercialism. Then as waves of industrialism, usually associated with sources of power (first steam, then gas and electricity, next oil and electronics) swept over the globe, the whole world became an international market.

The major social consequence of this shift from dominantly agricultural to mainly commercial-cum-industrial has been urbanization. Obviously, the very fact of increased population has had its say in this as well, for, where the population density worldwide was less than 20 per square kilometre in the early part of the twentieth century, it will be 60 per square kilometre by the early part of the twenty-first century. Without getting too involved in chicken-and-egg arguments about which came first, the coupling of more people and more industrialism jointly has an urbanizing effect.

At the time of World War II (1939–45) only three-tenths of the world population lived in towns, defined broadly as settlements of more than 5000 souls. At about the time of writing (1995) the balance is turning, and for the first time as many people are living in towns as in rural circumstances. By 2025 the three-tenths of 1945 will be three-fifths – urban dwellers will outnumber rural dwellers by six to four.

Again, one sees the developed nations leading where the rest of the world will follow. The early industrialized Britain witnessed that similar change during the reign of Queen Victoria (1837–1901) for that long-serving monarch began by ruling a nation in which the majority were rural residents and ended with a majority of urban residents. Close to 80 per cent of the European population is urbanized, where in medieval times the figure was less than 10 per cent; in the United Kingdom the 'urbanization' figure is close to 90 per cent (United Nations 1986).

Old and urban

Why is it necessary to emphasize the urban/rural axis so strongly? The reason is that it acts as an emblem of the new social conditions in which the new and larger groups of older people find themselves, and it betokens the kind of life they must perforce lead, not least the manner in which they are funded and otherwise supported. Few and mainly rural old people have become many and chiefly urban old people, and that, as we have seen, is a British, European and a global trend.

There are a number of characteristics to scrutinize. Urbanism plays its part in the drop in numbers of the younger age-groups. What is somewhat severely termed 'the labour value of children' declines, for one no longer needs children to maintain the domestic economy of localized and self-sufficient agriculture or small-time cottage trades. Put harshly, in urban conditions the child needs the adult more than the adult needs the child, whereas the reverse is broadly true in rural circumstances. Town life also tends to fracture family networks, so that social supports are less available; it has a more anonymous atmosphere.

That is not sentimentally to pretend that families were automatically more comfortably close-knit then; there is plenty of evidence of friction and rumpus in family circles in the past. But this move to town life leads to changes in the social apparatus. An example of this alternative urban scenario is the inclusion of more formal, often institutional, supports. The school, which helps care for the children while the parents work, is the most obvious example. Urbanism normally entails a separation of the home and the workplace, so that scenes such as Effie peacefully playing at the foot of Silas Marner's loom as he wove are much less frequent – although the electronic revolution may introduce something of the reverse effect, with an increase in working from home. Thus, a more institutional regime may mean, for the older person, the likes of the day centre or the residential care home (Midwinter 1990).

These are organic matters of human affairs, and as such they do not conform to cut and dried categories. Nevertheless, were one to draw a continuum with, at one end, older people in rural circumstances, informally cared for by families, and, at the other, older people in urban circumstances, formally cared for by state resources, such as pensions and services, then today's situation in the United Kingdom would edge toward the latter pole. Once more, it must be stressed that this is a neutral statement. Being cared for by one's family is not necessarily better than being cared for by the state, despite a good deal of syrupy nonsense having been claimed to that effect by those with a nostalgic 'Coronation Street' view of the past. There are many older people who may thank their lucky stars that they may enjoy the privacy of living alone on the proceeds of the state, instead of suffering endless humiliations and distress in crowded and unfriendly family settings.

It will be obvious that much of this analysis is about why towns grew rather than how. That is, they largely came into being at economic rather than social dictate. The classic case might be the factory, mine or mill attracting workers in huge numbers – by 1870 the average British work unit employed 200 people – into its close confines, and compacting housing around that worksite in similar cramped ranks. It is a question of density, or rather of three types of density, fitting together like the nesting of Russian dolls; more and more people pressed into ever more confined workplaces, situated in increasingly packed urban locales. With laconic elegance, the political scientist, Herman Finer (1994), entitled this concept 'congregation'. He identified it as an apt descriptor of western industrial society; it may be projected as a now and future world phenomenon.

Perhaps the most significant political outcome of these historical changes was on the bureaucratic front. Commercial and urban life demands much more formal approaches to law and regulation. Where an oral tradition of custom and rights (for which, incidentally, a modicum of older people was patently valuable) might have been sufficient for purely small-scale agri-cultural communities, the complexities of trade and town life required a much stricter and more codified regulo. The great sociologist, Max Weber (1983), described such developments as 'rationalization', and pointed them out in all forms of early modern western life.

One meaningful aspect of rationalization was a growing interest in signalling rites of passage by reference to particular birthdays. For centuries most people had no or but a hazy idea of their age, and for the most part it didn't matter. Old age, for instance, was more of an organic condition, relating either to a deterioration in physical and mental faculty, or, more happily, to the onset of silver-haired sagacity. There was – there still is – a generational connotation to this. The existence of the three-tiered family of grandparent, parent and child is the clearest illustration of this. In the film *The Savage Innocents*, with Anthony Quinn as the prototypical Eskimo, this generational effect was vividly underscored by his mother-in-law, who, once she was certain his wife was pregnant and the next generation assured, and after delivering herself of some useful homilies on childbirth and babycare, abandoned herself on an adjacent ice floe in the track of a hungry polar bear.

The official use of birthdays has grown apace, although it is, in historical time, a fairly recent practice. The 1837 Act for the Registration of Births, Deaths and Marriages was plainly a milestone in this regard, although during the preceding two or three centuries birthdays had begun to be used in professional, military and legal circles for, in illustration, access to particular posts. The use of the ages 21 and 60 became more constant, and by the time of the industrial revolution, many more people would have known their age than was the case a couple of hundred years previously. During this early modern era, 'stratification by age increased, the anomalies of youthful advancement everywhere reduced, and the redundancy of the elderly was increasingly emphasised' (Thomas 1977: 248).

Slowly, 60, 65 or 70 was adopted as the official threshold to old age. It may be not entirely coincidence that the initial payment of the old age pension in 1908, with 70 as the age of eligibility, came some 70 years after the registration of births' legislation, and was therefore the first point at which even a perfunctory check on applicants was possible. It is difficult to exaggerate the effect, much of it displeasing, which this intimate identification of older age with officiously determined birthdays has wrought.

Retirement

All of these factors mixed together create and characterize the phenomenon of retirement. The relative number of older people, the socioeconomic implications of urbanization, especially the use of more formal and institutional methods of social support, and the official deployment of birthdays all conjoin to instruct the scope and nature of retirement.

The central and overarching feature, however, was and is work. The technological changes of the past 150 or 200 years since the onset of the industrial revolution have had the effect of reducing the sheer amount of work. Up to that point, the entire non-aristocratic population, in Britain as across western Europe, would have been expected to work, with the exception of very tiny children and severely disabled or decrepit people. Child labour was not the invention of a dreadful industrialism; it had always existed in the fields and in the cottages of an earlier rural economy. Agriculture offers the perfect example. Ninety per cent of Britain's medieval population was engaged in agrarian activities, and nearly a third of the British workforce was still engaged in agriculture at the ascension to the throne of Queen Victoria. Now the industrialization of agriculture is such that less than 2 per cent of the workforce is able to produce a half of what a gluttonous country eats, which according to many medical commentators is more than we need.

In the armed forces, the powder monkeys, who scuttled across the blood-stained decks of British frigates at the battle of Trafalgar in 1805, would be at primary school today. Adults, with technical assistance, performed the analogous tasks in the naval battles of the two World Wars. By the Falkland and Saudi Arabian campaigns of the 1980s and 1990s, humans were scarcely required at all, so sophisticated had the mechanics of warfare become (Midwinter 1985).

Work has collapsed. The Victorian worker toiled up to 12 or 14 and even 16 hours a day for six days a week, with Good Friday and Christmas Day the only guaranteed holidays. The 1847 Ten-Hour-Act – although it only applied to women and young persons – helped, as did the initiation of the Saturday half-day. However that still meant working from 6 a.m. to 2 p.m., and the traditional Football League kick-off at 3 p.m. was governed by that timing. 1871 saw the introduction of the first bank holidays, while many were now down to a 55-hour week, with, the railway companies in the lead, the first instances of a paid week's holiday. Compare that with the 35-hour, five-day week, upward of 14 bank holidays, and typically 25 or 30 days' annual leave of many present-day contracts.

Nonetheless, these inroads were as nothing compared with those which took place fore and aft of the main working period. Swathes of time were subtracted from the old style workload by the expedients of delaying the starting age and bringing forward the finishing age of work. The notion of starting work in childhood, in some trades as toddlers, and of labouring until overtaken by death or decrepitude, has been replaced by education and retirement. Although it is customary to present these modes as pleasant and attractive, and in the case of education to urge that it involves some sort of investment for the future economy, it is not unduly sceptical to argue that both are primarily determined by the lack of available work. Many educational economists would claim, in more or less degree, that education is a consumer good, in that we have an elaborate educational system as the rewarding product of a rich and sophisticated economy, rather than to service that economy; it is effect rather than cause (see for example Bowman and Anderson 1963; Walters 1981).

It is similar with retirement, which is the consequence of an increasingly technological and decreasingly labour-oriented economy. The Victorian working man did not save for older age, not because he was feckless and not just because he might have had gloomy thoughts about his longevity, but because (and always accepting that he would have enough in his wages to allow such thrift) he expected to work until he dropped. The graudal increase in the school-leaving age – or, to grant it its realistic title, the work-starting age – from 10 or 11 via 13, 14, 15 to 16/18, with another three or more years' college life for a growing fraction, has been matched by first the invention of retirement – the work-finishing age – and second its gradual descent, official and real, down to the early 50s for many. If one could take an imaginary snapshot of the normal working span, *circa* 1840, of a man dying at 70, and one, also dying at 70, today, then one would find that the former worked one in three hours of his entire life and the latter one in 14 hours of his life.

That amazing decline in the all-round corpus of work does not take into account the underemployment and unemployment now apparently endemic in British and other economies. After a golden age of practically full employment from 1940 to 1975, the economy has resumed what seems to be its more natural character of having several million people either totally unemployed or in precarious tenure of employment. For some of them, that ratio of one to 14 hours would be considerably lengthened – although one should not forget that for some harassed souls these conditions of uncertainty lead to them working longer hours of work than the norm.

Although it was not unknown, especially in more upmarket professions, for men to retire gracefully, the history of retirement in any general sense dates only from 1859. In that year the Civil Service Superannuation Act was passed, albeit after much parliamentary coming and going over the previous hundred or so years, in respect of providing pensions for those in public administration. Based on the findings of the Northcote–Trevelyan Report (1855) on the civil service, it introduced a uniform service-based pension for those officers of the Crown at 60 years of age. That report significantly rejected the idea of flexible retirement, according to medical assessment, as cumbersome and invidious, opting for the arbitrary birthday as the touchstone. The bureaucrat had struck – it is somehow peculiarly appropriate that the civil service should invent the first major retirement scheme and that it should be for the civil service.

Other public agencies followed suit in slow procession, especially during the 1890s. Elementary schoolteachers, the police and other public servants, except for local government officers who had to wait until 1922, were next in line, while in the private sector, it was the big paternalistic firms, notably the railway companies, which kept the momentum rolling. Sixty, more frequently 65, was the birthday utilized, and the popular perception was reinforced that these ages indicated an unfittedness for work. The Northcote–Trevelyan Report (1855) said that 60 or 65 was the age at which 'bodily and mental vigour began to decline'. As in the civil service, there was usually an efficiency angle adopted among the other retirement sponsors, for a catch-all retirement age did ensure that the chronically incompetent might be weeded out without fuss, even if it meant many still capable people joined them. When the Liberal government, in the years before the 1914–18 war, introduced measures aimed at compensation for industrial injuries, this was a further spur, for employers believed that older workers were more vulnerable to accident. As an interesting gloss on that, one of the arguments against child labour had been the vulnerability of children to accident, and the consequent likelihood that adults might suffer allied injury (see Raphael 1964; Thane 1978).

In passing, it is worth recalling that the USA underwent a similar process and that, *mutatis mutandis*, all the industrial nations followed suit. As in the United Kingdom, it was really the last quarter of the nineteenth century when age discrimination 'grew virulently' at both ends of the age span, as American corporations strove to maximize their profitability. A species of pseudo-science argued the case for 'cumulative fatigue', and in the first decade of the twentieth century a working life of 15 to 65 years was generally adopted. In America, as in Britain, the ruling spirit was what was believed to be 'the productive potential', not any sentimental pap about cherishing the closing years of a loyal workforce (Graebner 1980).

Summary

The first step to an understanding of the current issues of retirement and income maintenance in retirement is the acceptance that old age and retirement are quite separate categories. There has always been a social factor of old age in practically every recorded society, whereas retirement, in any meaningful collective sense, is extremely new in historical time, no more than 100 or so years at the outside. Moreover the driving force in the implementation of retirement processes was work, or rather the pressure to ration or reduce the amount of work that people did, itself a consequence of industrial and post-industrial technology. The next step is an understanding of how society contrived to fund people who found themselves in this newfound category of 'retirement'.

2

The history of income maintenance for older people

Pensions and retirement

Retirement and pension – even the very words have been given a relatively new tweak, with the semantics of old age proving quite instructive. Used in anything like the present sense, retirement and pension are early modern coinages.

Retirement from office or business, usually having earned enough for the years ahead, then sometimes known as a 'competence', or being granted a pension, dates from the later seventeenth century, and the use of 'retired' in that context is early nineteenth-century in origin. A pension, in the narrower sense of an annuity or other payment to someone in respect of services, is older in style, but reaching only back into the sixteenth century. The services rendered were normally official, including payments to scientists and artists, and also royal favourites. In many cases then pensions enabled people to continue their work, rather than provided for them on its completion. That emphasis on a usually governmental provision is important, and initially the pensioner was frequently a state tool or mercenary. Samuel Johnson, forthright as ever, defined a pension as 'an allowance made to anyone without an equivalent. In England it is generally understood to mean pay given to a state hireling for treason to his country' (Johnson 1775). This was certainly the seventeenth and eighteenth-century view, although, more pleasingly, the eighteenth century also witnessed a softer focus, as 'pensioner' was deployed to describe those who had performed military service, normally having sustained injury, and who found themselves in the Greenwich and Chelsea Hospitals.

The first recorded public post-work pension was paid in 1684 to Martin Horsham, a land-waiter of the Port of London, when he grew 'soe much indisposed by a great melancholye' (Raphael 1964), and from about 1712 onwards, civil servants did benefit from various superannuation schemes. However, it was well into the nineteenth century before the two terms, retirement and pension, became popular parlance simply because the association of a monetary settlement for finished vocational services fell way outside the experience of all but a few officers.

It was to be the alliance of the two notions – retirement from paid work and being in receipt of a regular pension on so doing – which was to bring both words into prominence. If wholesale groups of workers were to be compulsorily retired at a given birthday, how were they supposed to fund the rest of their days? The answer, of course, was to be found in some kind of superannuation plan, and superannuation, since its coinage in the late seventeenth century, has consistently had that meaning of dismissal on account of age and what were thought to be its attendant infirmities.

Thus was born the concept of occupational pensions, to which one might make contributions during one's working life. Hitherto, arrangements had been much more ad hoc, rather after the manner of a benevolent fund which might arbitrarily pay out a little grant according to perceived need, available funds and even personal whim. Until the last 10 or 20 years, this use of a regular system of occupational pensions has been nowhere near comprehensive. It has been an advantage mainly enjoyed by state employees, both national and local, and, increasingly, larger firms with the capacity to introduce their own viable company schemes. Added to this were those who, through savings and investment, had contrived to provide for their older age. Like the majority of the occupational pensioners, these initially came from the middle and professional classes.

It is safe to say that, until comparatively recently, the process of funding one's older age from one's paid work, typically in the form of an occupational pension, was a middle-class practice, with the exception of some groups of craftsmen employed by very large companies. 'Getting a job with a pension' was something of a mantra chanted to the offspring of aspiring working-class parents from the 1930s to the 1960s; a pension was the shining emblem of having made it into middle-class status.

This youthfulness of occupational pensions must be stressed. Even among professional people outside of the public sector, the habit had been to work as long as possible in, characteristically, the family business, be it bakery or solicitor's office or whatever. The occupational pension is the other side of the medallion of general and regular retirement, which, as we have underlined, is barely 100 years old itself. The one was, and is, unnecessary without the other (Raphael 1964).

Old age and infirmity

Yet there has always been, in every society, older people who could not work because of debility and similar reasons, and who presumably had to be catered for in some fashion. Naturally it was supposed that the principal carers would be their families, an expectation which is still manifest today, but there were still those with no family or with no family able or willing to help. This gave rise to the second strand in the development of income maintenance for older people: provision out of the public purse, administered either locally or nationally. It is a much older strand than that relating to occupational pensions, in so far as the majority of the population have been concerned.

When Britain's economy was primarily agricultural and its communities relatively self-contained, alms-giving, processed by the ubiquitous church through its parish priests, monasteries and the like, was the main back-up, should family aid fail. It was necessarily sporadic, not least because the purpose of the donation was more to do with the giver than the receiver, the view being taken that alms-giving might influence the destiny of the donor's immortal soul. That flaw still exists where attempts are made to solve social problems by the spontaneity of voluntary effort; one cannot readily assure that the focus is rational or sharply defined enough.

As the British economy grew more commercialized, and the state more centralized, there was a definite sea change, with the sixteenth century seen by most commentators as the critical phase (see, for example Elton 1953). On the one hand, the shifts in economic practice were providing a different scale and fashion of improvidence. Trade and urban life meant a more unstable populace, with less steady allegiance to the land; beggars and vagrants were more likely to be on the march. On the other hand governmental powers vested for example in the Tudor monarchy and its authoritative privy council were able to make national prescriptions and make them stick. It is often forgotten that the ability to administer schemes is as important as the wit to invent them.

The 1601 Poor Law Act, the famed '43rd of Elizabeth I', proclaimed the first centralized policy for the relief of poverty. It was in effect the consolidation of a number of previous statutes, but it laid down in coherent format a strategy for England and Wales whereby each parish was obliged to organize poor relief. It did so principally through the office of the parish overseers, a title used first in 1572, who were appointed by the magistrates, those usually obedient servants of the monarchy. Poor rates could be levied by the overseers on the property within the parish, and these could be enforced by the magistrates, while the whole set-up was centrally watched over by the privy council.

There was thus extensive delegation, for in a time of unreliable communication it made sense to depend on localism. This made for some disparities of treatment – hence the nursery rhyme 'Hark, hark, the dogs do bark' with its recipe of variable reaction to beggars. Many will recall that, when 'the beggars have come to town, some gave them white bread and some gave them brown', while other places 'whipped them out of town'. Nonetheless, it was a national scheme. When the term 'the welfare state' is employed, it is worth remembering that 'state' is as significant in the epithet as 'welfare'. The state, then, has administered welfare since at least 1601, and this automatically embraced the aged poor.

For 300 years this system was sustained. Sometimes the central vigilance was firm – the Elizabethan period; during the Commonwealth period of Oliver Cromwell – sometimes it fell into desuetude – the early Stuart period; the eighteenth century – but it struggled on, each of the 15,000 parishes of England and Wales committed to its share of 'parochial laissez-faire'. Throughout this time, there was little need to adopt a high-profile definition of old people who were poor as opposed to anyone who was poor. It was a matter of doling out assistance to families and individuals who were pauperized (Roberts 1960).

From one angle this preserved a significant truth which the twentieth century has conspired to obscure by tending to associate old age and poverty, as though one were cause of the other. By lumping all the impoverished people together, the predecessors of the current social security system explicitly accepted that poverty was a structural rift throughout society. To put it in the simplest terms, and this remains true today, most poor old people had previously been poor young and middle-aged people. In those earlier centuries, poor old people normally had insecure and ill-paid employment; their families followed suit in that unhappy regard, and were able to offer much succour; they all probably found themselves in need of help from the parish overseers. Perhaps the single difference of note was that the aged poor would not have been feared as a possible public hazard as the more ablebodied vagrants often were.

The new poor law

The combined effects of congregation, of expanding population, growing industrialism and plentiful town life, began to overwhelm the old poor law system, even though the parish authorities of some of the new large cities, Manchester and Liverpool for instance, made reputable efforts to meet the needs of paupers. By the early decades of the nineteenth century, the parochial system was in some disarray; there were raised eyebrows at the mounting costs; and there were criticisms of the criteria in use. The Speenhamland system, adopted by the Berkshire magistrates in the late eighteenth century, is often quoted as an example of the then current mode, whereby the poor law authorities supplemented the income of people to a given level, the price of bread being deployed as the yardstick. This, it was said, encouraged employers to underpay and employees to underwork. The poverty trap is no new phenomenon.

The 1834 Poor Law Amendment Act is as significant a date in the story of welfare provision as 1601, or as 1942, the year of the publication of the seminal Beveridge Report (Beveridge 1942). Chiefly the brainchild of Edwin Chadwick, the most productive of the disciples of the Utilitarian political scientist, Jeremy Bentham, the new poor law must be seen as part of the administrative 'tutelle or guardianship'. This encompassed the erection of a tutelary state, by which it was hoped to clear the social arena of the obstacles, such as ill-health and crime and ignorance, which stood in the way of humans' exploitation of their personal self-interest. For it was the stance of the Utilitarians or Benthamites that 'the greatest happiness of the greatest number' lay in the total and harmonized expression of those many egoisms. An important aspect of this was the labour market, interfered with and destabilized by the synthetic protection of workers by the old poor law. The 'less eligibility' principle of the new regulation insisted that whatever a pauper received would be less than the meanest kind of employment, so that accepting poor relief would be a last resort; it would be 'less eligible' than the lowest paid job, and this, it was opined, would thrust men (and it was chiefly aimed at men) onto the labour mart.

It grandiosely missed the fundamental point that, in the new world of international trade, men and women were forced out of work, not so much by indolence, but by sudden and disruptive shifts in the national and global markets. Be that as it may, the very unpopular new poor law was introduced, with well-to-do ratepayers hopeful that inroads would be made into the vast sum of £6 million annually paid for the relief of pauperdom. The old parish structure was targeted and groups of parishes were merged into 'unions', single-purpose agencies which came to do much of the work we would now associate with local authorities. The unions, for example, were made responsible for the registration of births, deaths and marriages. Such 'vital statistics', a coinage of that era, were a valuable instrument in the hands of the Utilitarian reformers. Nationally, the poor law unions were supervised by the Poor Law Commission, later Board, although its vigilance was sometimes made a mockery of by the intransigence of local pragmatism. This offers a splendid illustration of what was to prove an enduring British device: the bipartite balance of a central ministry or department with semi-autonomous local agencies, summarized in the vernacular as Whitehall/town hall (Finer 1952).

Gradually local government was reformed in Britain, and many responsibilities were assumed by the burgeoning multidisciplinary authorities. The poor law unions were one of the last agencies to fall into the engulfing maw of these local authorities. The 1929 Local Government Act transferred their duties to the newly formed public assistance committees of the local authority. It was in 1934, with the economic depression of those years a stark reality, that the Unemployment Assistance Board was established to cope with the longer-term unemployed, with elderly people in need of welfare still left in the province of the public assistance committees.

To complete the administrative tale, World War II emphasized the need for a strong national voice in welfare provision, and then, as a plank in the post-war welfare state, the National Assistance Board was set up in 1948 to offer support to all social casualties on a nationwide basis. From that administrative angle, therefore, 1934 marked the formal separation of the working and the post-working population. Until that point, indigent people were treated alike; they were all, so to speak, impoverished and unemployed, irrespective of age and whether they might or could work again.

Poor relief and the pension

In terms of state monetary grants, the distinction between poor relief and pension was made somewhat earlier. Yet in so far as older people were treated differently than younger people, the crucial touchstone was infirmity; one constantly finds in the records the adjectives 'aged' and 'infirm' in conjunction. In fact, it was 1890 before ages were officially recorded for poor law purposes, with 65 normally adopted as the critical age. It is true that hitherto 60 had been utilized 'as the guiding line', and the poor law guardians (the locally elected members in charge of each poor law union) 'recommended that persons alleging themselves to be over 60 should not against their will be classified as able-bodied except with the approval of a medical officer' (Royal Commission on the Aged Poor 1895). Even at this stage the critical feature was whether you were 'able-bodied' and thereby fit for work, or 'infirm'. However, what has become known as the 'institutionalization of old age', by birthday as opposed to declining capacity and deteriorating health, really dates from this time.

By that same token, it is possible to offer reasonably reliable figures from this date. Taking 1892 as a typical example, some 268,000 people over the age of 65 were, on New Year's Day, in receipt of poor relief in England and Wales. Over a 12-month period ending Lady Day (25 March) 1892, 402,000 people over 65 had been treated. This was just under a third of the approximately 1.1 million over 65s living in England and Wales. By comparison, at the turn of the eighteenth century, with the old poor law still in operation, about 160,000 people over 60 – that is, close on a third of an over-60's population of 0.5 million – were annually the subject of parish relief (Royal Commission on the Aged Poor 1895).

Although the next chapter will discuss the story of relief in kind to older people and the general culture in which old age welfare has been proffered, it must be stated clearly here that the enormous majority of these older paupers were paid 'outdoor relief', that is, they were given a weekly allowance of money by the poor law union. Only something like a quarter of those older people in receipt of relief were in institutional care, notably in workhouse dormitories or poor law hospitals. In fact, in the 1890s, more than half of all the 'outdoor' paupers were over 65, testimony to the growing need for assistance among that age-range.

What must be stressed is the long tradition of monetary payments to older people in distress. It was not a new idea, and that was an essential part of the background against which the campaign for a national old age pension was mounted. It was argued, then as now, that pensions would ruin the economy, and even some trade unions and friendly societies, which had stoutly tried to bring some succour to working-class communities during the nineteenth century, were opposed. They felt, in yet another preview of modern debate, that wages should be sufficient for workers to make an independent provision for older age, and they were afraid that public assistance might, like the old Speenhamland system, actively depress wages.

Gradually both employees and employers came to acknowledge that a national pension scheme was necessary, as both sides came to recognize the changes in working practices described in Chapter 1. There were over a hundred ideas for pensions mooted as this debate waxed fiercely over several years and through dozens of commissions and enquiries, crucially the Chaplin and Hamilton Committees of the House of Commons. A major debating point was whether the pension should be contributory, with workers paying so much a week into some form of fund, as some of them had previously done as members of a friendly society. It is worth mentioning that in 1900 these mutual aid groups like the Oddfellows and the Foresters had six million members, at a time when the trade unions could muster only 1.3 million.

Eventually the non-contributory proposal of the social reformer Charles Booth was accepted. The Fabian Society (what anachronistically might have been called a left-wing think-tank), the trade unions and the friendly societies supported him. It would not be a direct tax on wages, whilst some workers might continue to pay into the friendly societies. The employers, who might also have been called upon to contribute and who were growing increasingly cautious about the costs and hazards of older workers, were also inclined to accept Booth's version.

Politically, the reforming Liberal government of 1906, mainly associated with the names of the prime minister, A.H. Asquith, and David Lloyd-George, was eager to show its social colours. Thus in 1908 a non-contributory weekly pension of five shillings (25p) was agreed. Any number of compromises were involved in the new statute. The planned eligibility age of 65 was abruptly and arbitrarily lifted to 70; rather exaggerated estimates suggested the cost would be £30 to £40 million a year, whereas a 70-year marker cut that annual bill to £8 million. Moreover, a sliding scale was introduced, whereby only those whose other annual income was not more than £21 could claim the entire bounty of 25p; by £31 it was reduced to a shilling (5p). There was a desperate concern, reflecting a mental set apparent from the sixteenth to the late twentieth centuries, that only the deserving poor would benefit. Claimants had to be British subjects of twenty years' residence, without a prison sentence in the last 10 years (and the 1898 Inebriates Act caught out a few luckless old people on that score), and neither lunatics nor on 'indoor' relief (Collins 1965; Thane 1978).

Despite these hurdles, 490,000 old people drew the first old age pension in January 1909. At that point there were some 1.5 million over-65s in England and Wales, of whom roughly a third obtained the new benefit. In admittedly very rounded terms, the situation was quite similar to what it had been in the early 1800s and in the 1890s, with approximately a third of the age-group in publicly assessed need of public support.

We arrive then to the first and great truth about the old age pension. Where the occupational pension is in direct line from the allocation of public monies to officials, the old age pension developed directly and unequivocally from the poor law. The old age pension was the nationalization of 'outdoor' poor relief.

The old age pension

What had been granted locally by the poor law unions was now granted by the state. Overnight, the number of old people receiving 'outdoor' relief was halved. The burden of their upkeep was simply transferred from the local poor rate to the national taxes.

In 1912 about 643,000 over-70s were drawing the old age pension. In 1896 26 per cent of people over 60 had been in receipt of 'outdoor' relief. By 1912 that figure had fallen dramatically to 16 per cent, the majority of them, one may properly suppose, aged between 60 and 70. With the help of other social reforms such as national insurance introduced by the Liberal government, the reduction of official 'pauperism' (as opposed, it must be understood, to poverty) was, in 1912 as compared to 1896, an astonishing 95 per cent, and obviously the poor rates were slashed accordingly. Equally plainly, what had occurred was the conveyance of a huge swathe of taxation from local to national sources.

This issue is even more pertinently underscored by reference to the actual value of the individual sums involved. From the time of the new poor law in the late 1830s, a fairly standard rate of payment to old paupers had emerged. Their 'pension' – and it is instructive that the word was in occasional use, preparing the way for its moment of total glory in 1908 – was between 13p and 15p a week, although it fell to 10p in the 1870s and 1880s, when cries about overexpenditure were loud, rising to 15p again in the decade before World War I. But, especially for old people living alone and heavily dependent, there were regular supplements throughout this time, occasionally in kind, but more often in cash. This meant that in the period 1837 to 1908, elderly paupers ordinarily received no less than two-thirds of the average adult working-class wage. Sometimes it was higher; even in the severe 1880s, it never dropped below a third.

The old age pension was increased in 1919 to 10 shillings (50p), but the poor law authorities were continuing to pay out supplements, as did their successors, the public assistance committees. These were needless to say paid to those older people whose dependence was greatest, but it often amounted to a further six shillings (30p). This brought the income of many up to two-thirds of the average manual wage, just as the poor relief had ordinarily contrived to do.

In the simplest terms, an elderly pauper living alone in 1908 might have swapped 'outdoor' relief of 15p for the old age pension of 25p, with the likelihood in either case of supplements of, say, 10p to 15p, at a time when the average wage, after deductions, was probably not much more than a pound or so. To bring the comparisons within reasonable living memory, when the old age pension was 50p in pre-war days, and the average working-class wage was around £2 to £3, one can quickly see that the ratio of one to the other was something above a quarter, with of course any resort to extra payment from the public assistance committee raising that to possibly a third (Thomson 1984).

In truth, the unsupplemented old age pension has never since its inauguration risen above two-fifths of the disposable income of the average manual worker, and, pre-empting Chapter 5, is now hovering below a third of that figure. Mention of supplements is also useful as a reminder that extra payments have always been necessary for those in the most dependent categories. The standard rates of neither the poor law authorities nor the old age pension agencies have been sufficient to permit the subsistence of those in the harshest circumstances; there has ever been a clutch of means-tested benefits for elderly people as there are today.

However the plain truth is that not only was the old age pension the generalized national replacement of the localized provision of poor relief for 'aged paupers'; it was scarcely, if at all, a real improvement upon the old dispensation.

The remainder of the story until the onset of post-war times may soon be told. Charles Booth had struck a highly civilized note with his progressive view of universal benefits; 'benefits which all enjoy have no slur', he claimed. However, the contributory approach, first mooted in 1879 and closely associated with the name of the Anglican social reformer, Canon Blackley, remained persuasive for many. The insurance principle, with workers overtly paying into the scheme and receiving the rewards, was considered to have ethical merit, and the trade unions changed their minds and began to embrace that view.

Crucially, it was the approach used to deal with poverty in the workforce, for the Liberal government's 1911 National Insurance Act was based on a mixed pattern of contributions from employees, employers and state, in return for which there were benefits for unemployment and ill-health. Thus was the infamous 'dole' invented, and, as with distress in old age, it was not a sufficient cover. Some workers – for example, badly paid workers who could not afford the contributions; workers whose job loss exceeded the statutory 26-week period – were thrown on to the mercies of the poor law guardians, later public assistance committees. That dual device – a standard allowance, eked out with a means-tested supplement – was unchanged as the leading characteristic of social welfare, and so it was to remain.

Nevertheless it was a step forward, and with family dependants added and with access to 'panel' doctors a critical feature, nearly half the population were, by the 1930s, enjoying National Insurance cover. In such a climate it was scarcely surprising that the old age pension would be subject to a similar change. The regulations had been relaxed, in part because the clerks found the detail of moral judgements difficult, and there had been 10,000 appeals in the first three months of the original scheme. One's age was now by far the premier and normally sole criterion. There were still, however, anxieties about costs, as well as worries about whether people were deserving. The annual expenditure on the old age pension was now over £25 million; over 90 per cent of recipients were on the full rate, nearly three-quarters of whom were women.

In 1925 the first move to a contributory plan was devised. The Old Age and Widows and Orphans Contributory Pensions Act was aimed at already insured men and their wives (women workers were still little regarded in these respects) and provided a bridge between a retirement age of 65 (it was reduced to 60 for women in 1940) and the state pensionable age of 70. This benefit was 50p, in line with the post-70 award, with widows also on 50p and orphans on 25p a week. In 1937 lower middle-class professions were included in the legislation, by which time well over 700,000 persons were in receipt of those bridging retirement pensions. From the point when the act became law to the outbreak of World War II, the number of non-contributory pensioners fell from one million to 500,000. The non-contributory pension was on the way out (Thane 1982).

Much of this activity must be assessed against an awareness of an economy often under severe pressure, especially as regards the great depression of the late 1920s and 1930s, with unemployment often running at disastrously high levels. It is during this period that, for the first time in any notable fashion, arguments were heard that, by lowering the age of retirement, room might be made for younger workers to enter the workforce, and this opinion carried some weight apropos the 1925 Old Age Contributory Pensions Act. The previous arguments had, as we have seen, chiefly involved the decreasing capacity of the older worker, unable any longer to manage the heavy toil associated with the docks or the mines. There was an analogue across the Atlantic, where retirement came by the 1920s to be viewed 'as a realistic antidote to unemployment', and where in the wake of the depression the 1935 Social Security Act, the hallmark of President Roosevelt's New Deal pro-gramme, involved 'the removal of people from the workforce'. During the tragically short interwar's era, the notion of retirement with pension at 65, as opposed to 'old age' provision for the aged infirm and/or impoverished, became quite firmly entrenched (Collins 1965; Graebner 1980).

As token of that, from a point just before the introduction of the old age pension in 1908 to the outbreak of World War II in 1939, the number of people over 65 receiving any public assistance or state pensions had risen from a third to two-thirds. That may be deemed a considerable advance, but the critics were ready to say that this meant that a third of older people had still to fend entirely for themselves.

3

The history of
old age welfare

Institutional care

Money is not the only method of supporting older people, although ordinarily
it is the most important one. There are also supports in kind, by way of services
or institutions, and these need to be taken into the reckoning when public
assistance for older people is examined. Furthermore, the nature of such
assistance, together with the monetary benefits, provides a key to the fashion
in which older people are regarded in society. Nor is it just the quantity of
money and other supports; it is the quality of them which vividly signals the
feelings the public harbours about old age. This is extremely significant, for it is
a circular process. Cheap provision, aridly presented, lowers public esteem and
evokes negative imagery, which in turn fuels the idea that tacky provision is
acceptable. Especially when these overall views come to be shared by the old
people themselves, this can have a detrimental effect on both the provision for
and the perception of older age – just as, conversely, an upwardly bounding
circle of high-quality amenities and positive outlook could have the reverse
effect.

The history of social welfare rehearses that combined approach; it has
normally been a mix of monetary hand-outs and help in kind. The monastic
alms-giving of medieval times was often accompanied by gifts of food
distributed, as the phrase was, 'at the gate', or on occasion delivered to the
homes of the poor, including, of course, the aged poor. Older widows were
permitted, as a form of welfare assistance, to glean the harvested fields of
medieval England. More tellingly for the longer run, there was the provision of
almshouses; for example there were four at Canterbury, two of them endowed
in 1084 by Archbishop Lanfranc in the aftermath of the Norman Conquest.
Usually administered by a priory from lay donations, normally in the shape of
tithes, they offered accommodation to the old and to the sick people of the

locality. These residential quarters were the forerunners of a long lineage of institutions offering non-domestic packages of care to indigent people. As medieval turned to early modern times, municipal authorities and merchant and craft guilds began to offer a more secular form of charity, but for many years the church remained the prime source of the relief of the poor.

Moreover, it is wrong to believe that the workhouse was a Victorian invention. From Tudor times there were some 'houses of industry', some 'workshops', some 'poorhouses', and, more particularly for the aged poor, some 'tenantries'. By the late eighteenth century London boasted a hundred or so poorhouses, hospitals and other welfare agencies, very many of them run as church-oriented charities. Although hospitals obviously had a cross-age clientele, older people have naturally remained among their main users, and any study of institutional provision for the elderly poor and sick should take account of that. The early English hospitals, such as London's St Bartholomew's (1123) and St Thomas's (1200) were founded as primarily nursing shelters, not least for old people. Their role was chiefly passive, for the physicians and surgeons of the age pursued their frightening craft from their home bases, and initially had little to do with the hospitals. It is no exaggeration to see the ancient almshouse as the predecessor of both workhouse and hospital (Midwinter 1994).

When the 1834 Poor Law Amendment Act obliged the 'unions' of parishes to establish workhouses, it was pushing at a door which was if not open then at least ajar. Many towns had had workhouses for many years, while nearly a hundred groups of parishes had, under earlier legislation, already opened 'union' workhouses. Old paupers had been included among the residents of these often harshly run premises. Nonetheless, after 1834 the workhouse pattern became nationwide, the aspiration being to drive ablebodied paupers on to the labour market by the ferocity of the workhouse regime, and to cut 'outdoor' relief as much as possible. By 1847 there were already over 700 workhouses in England and Wales, dedicated, through 'the Workhouse Test', to the eradication of idleness.

Unluckily, idleness and the need to force people to work was no more the problem then than it is now. As we noted in Chapter 2 it was chronic bouts of underemployment, both in the agricultural and the industrial areas, increasingly the consequence of difficulties with international markets, which caused poverty. Families could not care for themselves, let alone their older and less fit members. A workhouse patently could not cope with the distress resultant upon an entire town being thrown out of work. Furthermore, the plan to have workhouse 'classification', whereby there would be separate buildings or quarters for the 'classes' of pauper, was slow in implementation, primarily on the age-old grounds of seemingly exorbitant cost. The original poorhouses had been general and mixed, for instance, with a local parish throwing together its few orphans, its few ablebodied unemployed, its handful of 'idiots', its band of disabled people, maybe some other sick and impoverished souls, as well as its group of 'aged and infirm' parishioners.

The rationale of the 'union' workhouse was, through economies of scale, to arrange different accommodation, basically for children, ablebodied men, ablebodied women and old people. Although some of the larger towns and cities moved in this direction, enquiries as late as 1909 showed that precious little progress had been made. Moreover, it is hard to judge whether this was a good or a bad outcome. Where workhouses remained mixed, there were problems enough for old people tossed in with the rest of the social casualties of the locality. Where they were separated, it sometimes meant that husband and wife were kept apart.

This gave rise to one of the most bleakly potent emblems of aged pauperdom. 'It is Christmas day in the workhouse' (Sims 1903), perhaps the most well-known title of an English poem (except that many are wont to say 'was' Christmas day), rails at that injunction, while, when Albert Chevalier (1861–1923) sang his popular ditty, 'My old dutch' (We've been together now for forty years, and it don't seem a day too much'), he performed his turn against a workhouse drop-cloth, for it was pauper separation, not, as is sometimes now thought, death, which menaced the togetherness of Liza and Albert. Add to this the degrading stigma of the pauper burial, which affected the older pauper psychologically and emotionally, and the picture is, indeed, a gloomy one.

When, many years ago, I was researching the workhouse system, I was told by a very old clergyman how the church bells were not rung for a pauper's funeral and how the coffin could not be carried on the Queen's 'highway', which, he said, resulted in a circuitous journey from workhouse to cemetery to avoid the simple crossing of the highway which divided the one from the other. In truth, it was forbidden to separate couples where both were over 60, and at the poor law guardians' discretion where just one was; there was also evidence that 'there is no wish at all on the part of the married couple to live together' (Great Britain 1895). It also should be recalled that a main reason for marital separation, apart from the practical problem of what would now be called unisex dormitories, was birth control, lest more 'bastards' (such was the insensitive usage) might have to be funded by the poor rates.

It was exactly these sort of tales, some factual, some apocryphal, which heightened the sense of humiliation and disgrace felt by impoverished old people, and sombrely coloured the public perception of old age. In actual fact, the number of old people who found themselves in the workhouse was small, relative to the gruesome tales about incarceration therein. Throughout the period, the proportion of 'in' paupers was no more than a fifth to a quarter, and 'out' relief continued to be the principal means of treating the scourge of old age poverty. The same proportions held true for older people. During 1892, for example, of 400,000 older paupers offered any provision throughout that year, only 100,000 were 'indoor' paupers, the remainder being in receipt of 'outdoor' relief only. At any one time, about 60,000 'indoor' paupers over 65 were to be found, and a number of these were institutionalized for reasons of health only and not out of penury, for by now the great city poor law infirmaries, precursors of the important strand of municipal hospitals which were created before World War II, were doing a creditable job. What is interesting is that the figure of 60,000 'in' paupers over 65 constituted 4 per cent of the age-range – and the figure of people over 65 who are today in institutional care for health and social reasons is still about 5 per cent.

As the fine work of the poor law infirmaries indicated, there were improvements after about 1890, and by World War I it became more usual to use the term 'poor law institution' than the feared 'workhouse'. 'Indulgences' were offered to old people, by way of tobacco and snuff allowances or permission to enjoy days out of the workhouse. These were paternalistic in the extreme, with such 'indulgences' granted for merit and good behaviour. There was a gradual determination to erect special buildings for the 'worn-out sons of the state' (Crowther 1978); these self-evidently were the forerunners of the present-day local authority residential care homes. There were, of course, private nursing homes and rest-homes for old people from the well-to-do classes, but they were quite few in number and discreet in character; many wealthy people preferred to be catered for or nursed at home. In class terms, these agencies, *vis-à-vis* the workhouse 'aged' dormitories, parallel the occupational pension as against the poor law allowance, later old age pension (Finer 1952).

The equivocal view of old age

The mixture of allowances, as they were technically known, for about three-quarters of the aged poor and of rudimentary, often severe, accommodation for the other quarter, was for roughly 100 years the state's social policy. In essence, it did no more than recodify and formalize the system extant since Elizabethan times. The continuities in the treatment of old people down on their luck are quite startling.

It is fair to say that the Victorian administrator did not regard the aged pauper with the same dismay he did the ablebodied variety. In George R. Sims's (1903) doggerel monologue about Christmas day in the workhouse, the old man recalls the death of his wife the previous yuletide as, after refusing 'the house' with its rule of separation, she succumbs to starvation. He tells the guardians and their ladies what they can do with their Christmas dinner – the rude parodies which allude to this advice have some literary justification – but what is also telling is that the meal being provided is a substantial and appetizing one. Mayoral visitations on Christmas day nowadays to local residential homes as the elderly residents tuck into the seasonal fare are in the same tradition. The deference which accompanies it – what Sims called the 'thank 'ee kindly, mums' – perhaps remains part of the tradition.

What we are seeing is the playing out of an even lengthier and widespread tradition. If one looks at the way old people are treated throughout history and across geography, in all the societies that ever were and are, the overriding characteristic is ambivalence. This is attested by the historians of old age, principally by Georges Minois (1989), in his elegant history of attitudes to old age from ancient times to the Renaissance. He speaks of a switchback and counterpoint of feelings about old age, swinging from 'admiration' to 'contempt' and back again. He describes this movement eloquently as 'a capricious arabesque'. Sometimes a society or an individual will have greater respect for old age, and sometimes old age will be more likely to be ridiculed, but it is rare for one reaction to exclude the other for long.

Some commentators see in this equivocal response a fear of the coming encroachment of old age and death upon our own personages, but there can be no gainsaying the interplay of economic pressure. In another salutary reminder that domestic or family provision is not automatically preferable to institutional arrangements, there are many examples of such pressures. What anthropologists rather midly call 'death-hastening' processes have been prevalent in a world where resources have often been meagre and insufficient. As the redundant and less productive members of a family or tribal grouping, old people have often had to be sacrificed, sometimes literally. Georges Minois quotes the classical historian Herodotus on the Massagetae, an ancient folk-group of the northern Caucasus. Torn between finding their old people an economic burden and a fount of wisdom, they astutely compromised by ceremonially eating them, hopeful of ingesting both sustenance and sagacity; and it was 'held a misfortune not to have lived long enough to be sacrificed'. Whether the Massagetae termed this policy 'care in the community' is not recorded (Minois 1989: 11; Midwinter 1990).

That is a vivid instance of ambivalence, but there are echoes of it in Tudor England, with old people occasionally shoved out of their property by their aspiring and economically challenged younger brethren, just as there is evidence of Edwardian families in the East End of London edging their old folk towards the workhouse because of economic stress. These instances are an antidote to those optimists who look back to a golden age of living for older persons which was undermined by the onset of industrialism (Burgess 1962).

This ambivalent characteristic is apparent in British culture throughout its recorded history. Chaucer's fourteenth-century jokes at the expense of the old knight, January, and his young bride, May, have been repeated right through the ages to the music hall stages of the nineteenth century and the television sit-coms of the twentieth. As the names January and May remind us, the ritual division of the lifespan is of long-standing in sophisticated circles, and Shakespeare's seven ages of man, as described by Jacques in *As You Like It*, was but the lyrical portrayal of a then well-known model. Contemporary discussions of the 'third age' have echoes of the three and four division formats of medieval and early modern history. The four seasons or the four humours were sometimes so deployed, while one of several models of the threefold division was represented by the Magi – Gaspar: youth; Balthazar: middle age; Melchior: old age. Another model for this triple division was the Holy Family, with the baby Jesus, a youthful, even middle-aged Mary, and a stooping, aged Joseph. The utilization of Joseph is an interesting example of ambivalence, for he was at once the saintly figure of increasing contemplative wisdom, and the sidelined figure of decreasing physical attributes, even perhaps seen as bewildered by events and possibly impotent.

Within that undulating cultural wave one might perceive male and female differences. Where old men were seen as sexually inept, physically decaying and cautious with money and of opinion – the term 'fogey' has been attached to them since 1780 – old women have often been represented as the harbingers of evil, even unto witchcraft, with in medieval times epithets like 'crone' and 'hag' being deployed. Today it may be remarked that women still suffer more than men in respect of such negativity, not least because of an apprehension that sexuality declines more rapidly in the one than in the other; the dichotomy of the distinguished silver-haired, middle-aged male and the stylishly pretty, young, female television newsreaders has been used as an illustration of this. However, that is a variation on a central theme. In brief, 'traditional societies had a dual image of older people. They viewed old age as downward movement to debility, but also as upward movement toward knowledge and wisdom' (Covey 1989, see also Covey 1988).

A national culture of old age

As we move closer to our own era, we discover a much more standardized, coherent and dense manifestation of that dual imagery. From a national and popular viewpoint, the watershed of industrialism and urbanism was again critical. One major consequence was the increased rapidity of and coverage of communications, with the railway system the paramount element in that change. Indeed, until the coming of the railways, time was locally calculated, rather as we still have slightly varying lighting-up times today. Until the railways, no one travelled quickly or regularly enough to warrant the adoption of a national timing system, and it was 1884 before the Greenwich Mean Time convention was accepted. By the end of the nineteenth century, there were 20,000 miles of railway in place, carrying nearly 2.5 million passengers a day.

As well as the greater mobility of people, improved transport brought about a freer circulation of cultural manifestations, ranging from theatre companies to books and newspapers, themselves in cheaper and more abundant supply because of improved manufacture. With the abolition of such 'taxes on knowledge' as advertisement duty in 1853, stamp duty in 1855 and paper duty in 1861, British newspaper circulation rose from 39 million in 1836 to about four times that figure in the 1860s, and then, in 1896, the somewhat salacious *Lloyd's Weekly News* became the first newspaper to reach a million circulation. The number employed in the paper, printing and stationery trades sprang from some 90,000 in 1870 to well over 200,000 in 1901, and the annual output of new books jumped from 2000 a year in mid-century to 10,000 by 1900. Libraries, public and private (Mudie's, W.H. Smith's) were a coming vogue, and even before the advent of the great education acts dating from 1870, about three-quarters of the working classes were passably literate. There was a gradual extension in leisure provision, and some increase in the amount of money available to indulge such pleasures. Mass advertising had arrived; in 1900 shocked watchers were horrified to see the white cliffs of Dover daubed with a glaring advert for Quaker oats (Read 1979).

In a genuine sense, therefore, it might be argued that it was only after the 1830s that a deeply-etched *national* culture could exist, with a comprehensive and intensified set of values applied across all boundaries. Commentators may speak of Elizabethan drama and poetry as an illustration of 'English' literature, but in truth it was largely metropolitan in incidence and influence, with provincial manifestations severely limited on class and other grounds. *King Lear* is rightly quoted as a superb study of crumbling old age, but it remains true to state that, as to general social impact, more people watch a single episode of television's *Coronation Street*, which often has an 'old age' picture to convey, than have watched all the professional performances of *King Lear* since it was written. For the first time, the same cultural images of old age were common from Land's End to John O'Groats, as people read the same books and newspapers and watched the same theatricals. Pre-Victorian Britain was indeed ageist, but the ramifications of that ageism may have varied considerably according to local accident. The popular view of old age would henceforth be reproduced and reinforced on a unified footing.

The works of Charles Dickens may be taken as a tiny case study. Like few artists before or since, his appeal was extremely broad-based, attracting both critical and popular acclaim, with much evidence of family readings in middle-class homes and group readings in working-class districts. The penetration of the serialized family novel, upon which Dickens based his triumph, was all but total. In its first year of publication a Dickens novel would normally sell between 25,000 and 35,000 copies, whilst in just 12 years after his death, over four million copies of his books were sold on the home market; compare this amount with George Eliot's *Middlemarch*, much praised by the cognoscenti, which sold only 5000 of its cheaper edition in the months after its 1871 publication. One may safely assume that, apropos old age, Charles Dickens was a central player in the cultural process, as he was of all its facets. For example, witness his invention of 'the English Christmas' via *A Christmas Carol* and an annual series of other Christmas stories. He both replayed an imagery to his readers with which they were familiar and in which they believed, and by that reinforcement strengthened and coloured it.

Dickens used older people as harbingers of dark villainy and kindly eccentricity – for instance, the miserly wickedness of Ralph Nickleby and the fond, almost fey, benevolence of the Cheeryble brothers in *Nicholas Nickleby*. Another dualism might be Miss Havisham, a caricature of time-struck horror, and Mr Wemmick's aged parent, a dotty figure of harmless fun, both in *Great Expectations*. These standard traits are unrelieved by the steadfastness and valour associated with youth. Poignant illustrations might be the unselfishness of Little Nell or Little Dorrit against the narrow egocentricity of the former's grandfather and the latter's elderly father, while, in Ebenezer Scrooge, one finds a vicious miserliness and an odd and risible amiability in one and the same character. Dickens's older characters are usually either tight-lipped and hard – Mrs Clennam in *Little Dorrit* – or slightly crazed but amenable – Mr Dick in *David Copperfield*. In *Pickwick Papers*, in an amazing *tour de force*, Dickens wrote a picaresque novel of a young man, like Tom Jones, on his travels, but with the heart and soul of such a young adventurer embodied in an old gentleman, Mr Pickwick. The 'ageist' comedy arises entirely from that dysfunction of young mind in old body (see Ackroyd 1990).

As well as among his fellow 'family' novelists and their near neighbours the 'sensational' novelists, one can spot the same phenomenon in the aligned cultural elements. The new vogue for children's literature, for example, with Lewis Carroll the originating genius, shared some of this same 'bifocal' view of old age. In Carroll's characterizations of Father William, the White Knight or the Duchess, one finds a wavering between the threatening and the clownishly dim; sometimes the old characters are the cause of merriment and sometimes of dismay. Folk tales in translations – the Brothers Grimm, Hans Christian Andersen, the Arabian Nights – were coming on stream, and a moment's reflection will demonstrate how they too exhibited ambivalence – Red Riding

Hood's grandmother or the cruel stepmother of several plots – in respect of elderly people.

One might also look to the stage. After the Dickensian fashion the popular melodrama, perhaps performed by the sort of fit-up theatre managed by Vincent Crummles of *Nicholas Nickleby*, featured the sunken old dodderer, his mortgage foreclosed, or the lecherous old noodle, eyeing the comely heroine lasciviously. More significantly, the Savoyard comic operas of Gilbert and Sullivan embraced a form of urban ballad-opera which transformed the British theatre and became the nation's, in fact the world's, first light musical 'industry'. Their impact was phenomenal. By the time of Sullivan's death in 1900 there had been 36,000 professional performances of the operettas, as well as a major line in sheet music, songbooks and band-parts for a huge audience at home and abroad. Most librettos included an older, unattractive woman, often a fierce harridan who amused because of her hapless fondness for the young hero.

The image of fading and desperate romance was mirrored in that other forcing-house of cultural valuation, the music hall, where Dan Leno, most celebrated of pantomime dames, inaugurated the lineage of the impersonation of the older, ugly female. The emphasis was again of failing charms and seemingly inappropriate feelings, with a corresponding mix of derision and pity elicited from the audience. Like Dickens, both Gilbert and Sullivan and the pantomime art-form deliberately made their appeal to a cross-class audience and presented socially integrated work. People of all ranks of society, as well as in all parts of the country, were open to these rich influences. As Gilbert, a lover of the culinary metaphor, remarked, 'tripe and onions' and 'sweetbread and truffles' might alternatively dismay or satisfy the stalls and the pit, but 'a plain leg of mutton and boiled potatoes . . . is the most stable fare of all'. Those roles of the older woman whose life had passed by coupled with the older man of rather lewd and distasteful demeanour were sustained as, in common parlance, the unattractive old woman and the dirty old man, often evoking both detestation and sympathy in the same characterization. These were the cultural role models which would be boldly passed on to the cinema, radio and television of the twentieth century (Midwinter 1986).

Moreover, the Victorian values of bourgeois confidence and resolve probably entered the equation. Strength and power came to be adored, especially when related to business, military and imperial zeal, or sport. Such success, identified with crude versions of Social Darwinism and an eagerness to be seen as representing what the social commentator Herbert Spencer termed 'the survival of the fittest', was necessarily associated with youthful and middle-aged determination and potency. Weakness and frailty, overtly identified with old people, was to be avoided, if not altogether despised, for some obligation fell on the strong to protect the weak. Something of the same ambiguity may be observed in the Victorian bourgeois male attitude toward women – again the novels of Charles Dickens, pantomime and the comic operas of Gilbert and Sullivan offer picturesque testimony – where ardent affection and chivalrous but resigned protectiveness rest in equal measure. 'You silly goose' is a typical nineteenth-century epithet, combining emotions of both affectionate wonderment and a sense of female scatterbrainedness.

After all, Victorian expert opinion had it that the female brain was smaller and thus inferior to that of the male, making women subject to 'diseases of excitement'. The notion that frailty might encompass the virtues of placid contemplation, which for instance had caused the medieval mind sometimes to think better of old age, was far less acceptable in the tough, go-getting climate of Victorian England. This pronounced emphasis on the heroic virtues of intrepidness and daring was accepted wholesale.

The interplay of cultural perception and special policy is telling, if intangible. Impossible to quantify, it nonetheless pervades the atmosphere in which political debate occurs. What is certain is that, in both funding and services, ambivalence reigned. Primarily, there *was* provision, its rationale an uneasy sense that poor old people were somehow more to be pitied than blamed, as opposed to poor younger people who might be held culpable. Yet they were less important, because less productive and less powerful, than other younger people, those who were working hard, making profits, fighting for Queen and country, and colonizing. It is fair to claim that such a view was widely accepted by the British public, at least until the outbreak of World War II, and that it highly coloured the treatment of old people in the civil realm.

PART II

Present conditional: Post-work people today

4

Old age and retirement today

The ageing of Britain

A thousand years of British practice, a mix of grants in cash and kind for old people in a deeply ambivalent climate apropos ageing, brings us to the threshold of modern times, marked, with good reason, by the onset of the Second World War (1939–45). It was in the post-war period that the age-profile of Britain veered toward older age. What is sometimes rather glumly referred to as the greying of the population occurred, and this has now been blessed with the more cheerful label of the third age. At bottom, this usage sees the lifecycle in terms of status rather than birthdays. The first age is the phase of childhood and socialization; the second age is the phase of working and family-raising; and the third age is the post-work, post-familial stage. More controversially, a fourth age of dependent older age is also postulated, but for immediate purposes the triple division will suffice.

Although this concentration on status rather than chronological age is a valuable qualitative device, it still must be presented quantitively in figures which relate to ages. Peter Laslett, chief originator of the third age theme, has calculated a Third Age Indicator (3AI), based on the probability of those in a given population who are 25 reaching 70 years of age, and where 10 per cent of that population are over 65. The 3AI is an estimate of how many, having reached the second age, will survive to the third. By the 1950s it was 0.532 for men and 0.695 for women; that is, men had a chance of 532 out of 1000 and women 695 out of 1000 of reaching their seventieth birthdays. A 3AI of 0.5 is regarded as the criterion of third age attainment, and as the percentage of Britons over 65 had also reached 10.9 by 1951, it was evident that 'this date must be regarded as that of the emergence of the Third Age in Britain' (Laslett 1984: 379–89).

One or two comparisons might be in order. On the one hand, in the middle of the sixteenth century the 3AI was roughly 0.3, meaning that about a third of those who were 25 would survive until they were 70 – much less than now of course, but one suspects rather more than many people would guess, given the rather gloomy view usually held about longevity in historic Britain. On the other hand it is worth noting when fellow-nations emerged as third age countries. Using the male 3AI, and recognizing that ordinarily women survive more vigorously, Sweden and New Zealand just about tipped the crucial 0.5 scale by 1900; Norway, Denmark, Australia, the Netherlands and Italy reached this point by the outbreak of World War II; the United States and France were on a par with the United Kingdom; while it was nearer 1960 before the likes of Hungary, the then West Germany, Sri Lanka, Japan and Mexico touched the magic number of 0.5; China reached the same point in about 1980. It might be argued that by the end of the twentieth century much of the world will, as regards the third age, be as Sweden was in 1900 and Britain in 1950.

Putting the British figures into harder tack, and out of a population of 50.5 million in 1951, there were exactly 5.5 million who were over 65. By 1971, with the total population now 55.9 million, the over-65s numbered 7.3 million. The percentage had risen from 10.9 to 13 per cent, establishing a trend of rising proportions of older people. Conversely, the ratio of younger people was scarcely changing, the percentage of under-16s having moved in that time only from 24 to 26 per cent, a figure which proved to be the high watermark for post-war youngsters. Another way of describing these circumstances is by use of the not very beautiful term, the gerontic dependency ratio. This is the ratio of those of pensionable age against the adult group of women aged 20 to 59 years and men aged 20 to 64. In 1901 this ratio was 12:100; it was 34:100 in 1981; it is expected to be 39:100 in 2021.

An educational health warning should be added. Some commentators have made undue play of this trebling of the older/younger adult ratio, spreading alarming news about the rising problem of fewer workers maintaining more pensioners. That is not automatically bound to be the case; many have become pensioners in the wake of rising productivity gained through technological advance and an associated quieter demand for labour. It is the value of the amount of work done, not the number of people doing it, which is the more critical, and given what has been called 'the complex shifting patterns of labour force participation' (Johnson and Falkingham 1992: 45), it would be misleading to draw immediate economic and financial conclusions from an admittedly dramatic uplift in the gerontic dependency ratio.

By way of further breakdown, it might be useful for future reference to look a little more closely at the older population of Britain in the two or three decades after World War II. Taking a broader band of those over 55, who totalled 10.6 million in 1951 and 13.9 million in 1971, women continued to outnumber men in the ratio of roughly 3:2, while the life expectancy had also, needless to say, risen. Where at birth the male life expectancy in 1911 had been 51 (female: 55) it was, by 1961, 68 (female: 73). However, it is again worth referring to the issue of survival as opposed to longevity. A man in 1911 who reached 60 had a life expectancy of 14 years (female: nearly 16). In 1961 that had only increased to 15 years (female: a healthier 19) (Carnegie Inquiry 1993). These statistics may give some idea of the character of ageing in the immediate post-war era, but, as ever, an equally significant issue was the character of their working status.

The golden age

The period from about 1940 to about 1975 has been designated 'the golden age' by Eric Hobsbawm (1994), one of its most critically acclaimed historians. It was the stability of that period, rather than its affluence, which prompts endorsement of that appellation. Pre-empting, for the moment, the detailed review of Chapter 5, the post-war welfare settlement included the only genuine increase, unrelated to prices or wages, of the old age pension, and even though that was rather small beer, it did amount to a comprehensive subsistence allowance for the nation's elderly people over the next few decades.

The more important factor was the maintenance of full employment. The post-war welfare legislation, including that relating to pensions, was predicated on full employment, and it was the success of this policy which made for a considerable measure of serenity in the socioeconomic life of Britain, and indeed many other developed nations. Of course there were ups and downs, several of which seemed serious at the time. In retrospect, compared with what came fore and aft of that period, they were scarcely critical. If one looks at the distress of the great depression of the late 1920s and early 1930s, or the double recessions of the late 1970s and the late 1980s, then that middle era was calm enough in all conscience.

Before 1940 and since 1975, unemployment, plus underemployment in all its manifestations of short-time, part-time, temporary, contractural and allied devices, was, and is, the order of the labouring day. Where workers such as dockers might have been arbitrarily picked for work on a day by day basis in the bad old days, many are now plunged into week by week or month by month uncertainty about their paid work. Thus from 1940 to 1975 – the years are approximate frontiers – there was a kind of certainty about work which had been unknown, assuredly since the sixteenth century in Britain if not before, and which sadly has vanished again after an all too brief respite. The effect of this on retirement has, naturally enough, been profound.

It is often forgotten that the woes of the pre-war slump were not over until 1940. During the early months of World War II unemployment still stood at over a million, not having recovered from the devastating upheaval which had seen many millions out of work. The policy of so-called 'war socialism' involved an intense utilization and direction of labour, not only in terms of conscription into the armed forces, but for a wide range of war-associated civilian tasks. Total war meant total employment.

This was maintained after 1945. Although demobilization was organized rapidly and although the Japanese War, courtesy of the atomic bomb, was concluded some 15 months sooner than expected, the switch back to a peacetime economy was efficiently arranged. For example, there were 3,887,000 war-workers as the war in Europe ended in the late spring of 1945; a year later only 717,000 remained in such jobs. The national infrastructure,

especially in terms of the building industry, required substantial reconstruc-
tion. Neglected through the grim and funds-starved 1930s and then blitzed in
the war, there was much to be done to restore the national fabric, social as well
as economic. The war had also nurtured fledgling industries such as aircraft
production and chemical manufacturers.

Thus the post-war era saw a compound of the old – some resurgence of
coal-mining, ship-building and so on – with the new, along with extended
public service employment. 'Work or want' was the succinct slogan of the
massive export drive of the late 1940s, and such was the pressure on the labour
mart, there were appeals to older workers, pleading with them 'to continue in
their work a little longer rather than give up their routine and sink into
premature old age'. Now the medical hazards of foregoing work were stressed,
a reversal of the previous message that work in older age might be harmful and
retirement beneficial and a decent reward for 'the veterans of industry'. It was
a striking example that work was king, with its reign dictating whatever
justification was deemed necessary (Phillipson 1982).

Coupled with this was a decidedly Keynesian approach to economic
management and a general view, which wartime victory had affirmed, that
planning was the correct approach. The economic strategy of John Maynard
Keynes, around which a general consensus gathered in this period, retained
full employment as a major priority. If during these years the unemployment
figures touched 300,000, there were political tremors. Keynes argued that the
government should utilize fiscal levers such as interest and exchange rates or
taxation to keep the economy steady, using budget deficits to stimulate
demand in recession and budget surpluses to quieten demand in boom. There
were other helpful factors. Until the early 1960s, national service, usually of
two years' duration in the armed forces, meant that the entire ablebodied male
18 plus group was dried up out of the labour market like blotting-paper. This
was precisely the group which later was to pose the gravest problems with
employment.

In this situation, where the harmony of full employment and comprehensive welfare cover resulted in a steady state, the issue of retirement was as a
consequence resolved and settled. The age of 65 became the accepted year of
male retirement, save where in professions like the civil service there had been
an option for 60, which was also the ordinary point at which women retired.
Taking even a late juncture in the period – 1973 – one observes the truth of
this. Ninety-four per cent of adult males were economically active, and this
percentage of 94 per cent stood firm even for the 55–59 group. The figure
remained as high as 85 per cent in the 60–64 group, but dropped sharply at and
after 65 to as little as 19 per cent. Less than a fifth of men remained in work
after 65, even in this period of great economic activity. Many of these were
self-employed and in businesses and crafts where age was not regarded as a
limitation.

It will be remembered that in 1900 two out of three men were at work
beyond 65 – in 1881 it had been as many as three out of four – and that it was
still one in three in 1939, at all of which dates unemployment was rife. Now it
was less than one in five. The cut-off point of 65 was dramatic. Work between
60 and 65 was still at a substantial level, only 7 per cent below the national

working average of 94 per cent. Abruptly, the precipitous fall at 65 occurred. In the period 1940–75 everybody certainly worked, but at 65 everybody, almost everybody stopped. By 1990 only one man in 20 aged 65 or more was working, and, of these, only a third worked full time.

The statistics for women were different, reflecting a situation where, after the intensified use of female workers during the war, there had been some reversion to the older ways. During the early 1970s 74 per cent of all unmarried women were economically active (55 per cent for married), with a negligible number registered as unemployed. The remainder was classed as housewives and mothers. Thirty-four per cent remained at work between the ages of 60 and 64 (25 per cent for married women), and a mere 6 per cent (8 per cent married) after the age of 65. Taken together, one may estimate that only about 800,000 people (500,000 men; 300,000 women) over 65 were working in the early 1970s.

A glance at the overall statistics for the labour force in 1971 reveals that it mustered, in sum, 25 million people, made up of over 15 million men and just over 9 million women. For future reference, the age of 55 will become a useful yardstick; in 1971 the under-55s at work numbered 20 million, the over-55s at work but 5 million, roughly 3.2 million men and 1.7 million women. That was to be something of a peak for employment in the United Kingdom. Moreover, of the 8.4 million people of pensionable age (65 for men; 60 for women) only 1.3 million were still in employ, about an eighth. The rest – some seven million – were, whether they wished to be or not, already in retirement, (The Carnegie Inquiry into the Third Age Final Report 1993).

The coming of age

So to the last quarter of this century, a period characterized by a continuing, but not dramatic, surge in the survival of older people, alongside a much greater fluidity in working patterns. The best available estimates for the end of the century suggest that in 2001 the population of the United Kingdom will be 59 million, as opposed to 56 million in 1971. Of these, 15.4 million will be over 55 (1971: 14 million) and 9.2 million over 65 (1971: 7.3 million). Presented as proportions, the changes since 1971 might be seen as follows:

Under 16	1971	26%	2001	21%
16–64	1971	62%	2001	63%
Over 65	1971	14%	2001	16%

Once again the constancy of that middle figure – very approximately, the second age of working and parenting – must be noted. It is really remarkable that that figure of about three-fifths has remained constant since at least 1841, when it was exactly 60 per cent, but when the young fraction was 36 per cent and the old fraction only 4 per cent. The shifts have continued to occur in the two 'dependent' age-groups, young and old, leaving the mainstream population relatively unaltered. The forward estimates for 2031, when the total populace is supposed to reach 61 million, intimate that this middle group will then stand at 60 per cent, with 20 per cent in the younger and 20 per cent in the older brackets. This consistent configuration of the 'independent' population is

Table 4.1   Younger and older pensionable age-groups: United Kingdom, 1994

Age	Female (millions)	Male (millions)	All (millions)	Per cent
60–64	1.1	–	1.1	10.5
65–69	1.4	1.0	2.4	24
70–74	1.5	1.2	2.7	26
interim total	**4.0**	**2.2**	**6.2**	**60.5**
75–79	1.1	0.7	1.8	16.5
80–84	0.9	0.5	1.4	13
85–89	0.5	0.2	0.7	7
90+	0.2	0.05	0.25	3
interim total	**2.7**	**1.45**	**4.15**	**39.5**
Total	**6.7**	**3.65**	**10.35**	**100.0**

Source: Central Statistical Office 1995a

infrequently remarked upon and perhaps should have more bearing on social policy than has been the case.

The steady growth in the number of older people is chiefly explained by improving survival rates. This is reflected even in the comparatively brief time since the early 1970s. Men aged 50 at that time might have expected a further 23.3 years of life (women: 28.6) and men of 75 a further 7.4 years (women: 9.7). By 2001 that will have increased to 27.2 years for men of 50 (women: 31.6) and 9.2 for men of 75 (women: 11.8). The better chances of female longevity result in a gender imbalance, with, in the over-65 category, about 70 men to every 100 women. There are now some 6.7 million female and over 3.5 million male state pensioners, a total of 10.35 million in all. The figures for the last half of the century, whilst very satisfactory, are not as spectacular as those for the first half. The journalistic talk about older age, with a demographic time-bomb waiting to explode, is sadly misjudged – if explosion there was, it went bang by 1950, and the rest has been predictable fall-out and after-shock (Carnegie Inquiry 1993).

Let us consider how those of pensionable age are divided into younger and older groupings, as of 1994, bearing in mind the important fact that 568,000 new claims for retirement pensions were made during the year in question. In rough figures, each current year sees over half a million people added to the pension registers, while there are approximately 520,000 deaths of people over 65 (Table 4.1).

It will be of interest for present and future reference to have at hand the third age figures, defined as the post-55 age-range, divided by marital status, and using 1991 census figures (Table 4.2). Of that 14.84 million, 1.18 million are single, 9.1 million are married, 3.91 million are widowed, and 0.65 million are divorced or separated. With 5.77 million aged 55 to 64, 5.08 million aged 65 to 74, and just short of 4 million aged 75 and over, it will be observed that there is

Table 4.2   The over-55 population by age, gender and marital status: United Kingdom, 1991

Age/status	Female (millions)	Male (millions)	All (millions)
55–59			
single	0.08	0.1	0.18
married	1.1	1.2	2.3
widowed	0.2	0.04	0.24
divorced/sep.	0.1	0.1	0.2
	1.48	**1.44**	**2.92**
60–64			
single	0.1	0.1	0.2
married	1.0	1.1	2.1
widowed	0.3	0.07	0.37
divorced/sep.	0.1	0.08	0.18
	1.5	**1.35**	**2.85**
65–74			
single	0.2	0.2	0.4
married	1.5	1.8	3.3
widowed	1.0	0.2	1.2
divorced/sep.	0.1	0.08	0.18
	2.8	**2.28**	**5.08**
75+			
single	0.3	0.1	0.4
married	0.6	0.8	1.4
widowed	1.7	0.4	2.1
divorced/sep.	0.06	0.03	0.09
	2.66	**1.33**	**3.99**
Total	**8.44**	**6.40**	**14.84**

Source: Central Statistical Office 1995a

much less taper in the population pyramid than hitherto. The base is much narrower – 673,000 live births in 1993 as compared with 1,095,000 in 1900 – whilst the peak is, so to say, wider, so much so that some demographers have been inclined to use the analogue of the box-kite as a substitute for the old-style pyramid.

In summary, the over-55 population of the United Kingdom has grown by 1.4 million or 10 per cent since 1971 to its 1995 total of 14.84 million, while it is cautionary to recall that the over-55 echelon has only added marginally, no more than 1 per cent, to the fraction of the whole population it represented in 1971, namely, 25 per cent.

The new old age and work[1]

The critical question, however, relates to the status of this burgeoning band of older people, this 26 per cent of the total populace, the majority of whom may be considered to be in the third age. It is not so much how old they are, as what they do. In short, how many are retired?

The background to an answer to this query lies in the economic instability of the last 20 or so years. The national economies of the 'crisis decades' found themselves struggling to secure and defend the advantages of the post-war boom. The oil crisis of 1973–74, when the price of that increasingly important fuel quadrupled, appeared to trigger a world recession of long-standing. The globalization of the world economy in trading and manufacturing terms was matched by massive reductions in the national control over the movement of capital. International finance operated in a free market, and the well-tried Keynesian national levers of interest and exchange rates were no longer as operable or, truth to tell, for the many neo-liberal governments of the world, as desirable.

In Britain, where, as in most developed nations, both economic growth and public expenditure, especially on welfare elements, has become regarded as inviolate, there was depression and distress. Average annual growth of 3 per cent during the golden age dropped to 1 per cent in the crisis decades, and inflation, taking as a base a retail price index of 100 in the prosperous days of 1962, had flown to 1000 by 1992, when it began to stabilize somewhat, with the fight against it now regarded as a more important priority than full employment. The staple manufacturing industries of Great Britain almost vanished; the proportion of the workforce in such industries had remained at 48 per cent throughout the century, but now fell below 30 per cent and continued to drop. It was argued that the mismatch of a new 'techno-system' with outmoded business practice and institutions was a salient factor; just as the 1930s' slump had been identified with the switch from coal to oil, now the new wine of electronics was cracking the old bottles of economic organization. It might be added that, generally speaking, older workers were less well-placed to requalify themselves for this brave new world of computerized technology.

The collapse of work continued. The combination of old and new industries which had sustained post-war employment was disappearing, with the old trades vanishing all but completely and the new businesses becoming much less labour-intensive. This was in part because of the giddy cavalcade of technological invention with, so to say, the microchip on every recipe, and also because the abrasive stress of the global market enforced a leanness in labour requirements. During the more prosperous years, jobs had been well nigh artificially created for fiscal as well as social reasons, many of them in the public sector. Between 1961 and 1974, for example, the numbers employed in the education and health services rose from 1.7 to 3 million – it should not be forgotten that governments invest in as well as cut services for economic reasons. After 1974 the climate was all for shake-out and savings on labour costs (see Tylecote 1992; Hobsbawm 1994; Hutton 1994).

To some degree, the diminishing corpus of work had been disguised by the

Table 4.3   Older employment by age and gender: United Kingdom, 1973 and 1992

	Per cent of age-group employed – men				*Per cent of age-group employed – women*			
	55–59	*60–64*	*65–69*	*70+*	*55–59*	*60–64*	*65–69*	*70+*
1973	91	80	29	10	51	25	5	3
1992	68	40	15	6	56	24	4	2

Source: Trinder *et al*. 1992

progressive reduction in hours, itself a facet of the good times. Full employment in the nineteenth century, as we have noted, would have involved workers toiling for 60 and 70 hours a week, with few holidays. Full employment in the mid-twentieth century involved employees working 40 and 35 hours a week, with, by the 1970s, annual holidays averaging 20 to 25 days a year. The sum of all those hours and days represented a huge diminution of the actual time expended on work.

It might be said without undue simplification that employment fell for reasons good and bad. What is patently obvious however is that whatever the grounds the major beneficiaries or, according to personal judgement, sufferers, were the young and the old age-groups. The raising of the school leaving age, first to 15 and then to 16, in the post-war era, coupled with an immense expansion in further and higher education, reduced, whatever its other effects, a pressing demand on the labour market. At the other end of the lifespan, the joint action of late redundancies and early retirements took its toll, and the automatic termination of work at 60 or 65 was no more.

It is now that the reference throughout the text to 55 years of age as a touchstone becomes useful, for the men and women affected by these recent changes find themselves permanently out of work much earlier than 60 or 65. Indeed, there is evidence of those under 55 suffering, but 55 serves as a reasonable yardstick. Let us first look at the deterioration of older employment since the 1970s (Table 4.3).

The employment of men over the pensionable age of 65 actually rose a little from a low of 12 per cent in 1988 (men aged 65–69) to 15 per cent partly because of a slight upturn in the economy and partly because the earnings rule for state pensioners, whereby earned income might reduce the pension, was abolished. This is a further instance of the marginal rises and falls along an undulating track upon which the direction is fairly certain – overall, it is the drop from 29 per cent in 1973 which is significant. As for men under 65, it was the 1980s which witnessed the fastest plunge in their economic fortunes. In total, economically active men aged 55–65 numbered over 90 per cent in the early 1970s, and less than 65 per cent in the 1990s, a decrease approaching a third.

The situation for women seems to be much more stable. This masks some turmoil within the ranks of female employment, for the outcome represents a friction between the traditionally low number of older women working and the newer convention of more women working. With women much more

Table 4.4   The drop in older employment: United Kingdom, 1971 and 1991

	55–59		60–64		65+		Total
1971	71%	2.3m	54%	1.7m	11%	0.8m	4.8m
1991	67%	1.9m	39%	1.1m	3%	0.5m	3.5m
Absolute drop		0.4m		0.6m		0.3m	1.3m

Source: Trinder *et al.* 1992

extensively in search of work, the decline in the female section of the labour force is less noticeable, but is still present.

In real numbers, the number of men working and aged over 55 fell from 3.2 million in 1971 to 2.1 million in 1991, and the number of working women of similar age from 1.7 million to 1.3 million; in all-round terms, that constitutes a fall from 4.8 million to 3.5 million, a matter of 1.3 million, or 30 per cent. Aligning percentages and numbers, Table 4.4 shows a drop in absolute numbers.

Shades of retirement

There are several interim comments to add to those bald figures. Despite the high profile of the distinguished elder statesman or veteran entertainer, those who go on working after the state pensionable age, men or women, are more likely to be in low-skilled or unskilled jobs, and there is a relatively large amount of casual and part-time work, much of it self-employed. For instance, two-thirds of workers over 65 are part-time, compared with only 6 per cent of those working in the 50–64 age bracket, and jobs in agriculture and private or domestic service rate high among the older group. This demonstrates, of course, the compulsory tenor of retirement in the more organized and large-scale professions and services, but also what has been entitled the 'push' or 'pull' factor of the occupational pension, the latter exhibited by the lack of such a pension operating to retain, for example, low-skilled, self-employed workers in the workforce. Many, without doubt, welcome the push factor, and are only too pleased to accept premature or standard retirement supplemented with a decent occupational pension and possibly redundancy payments.

Retirement, then, has its metaphorical equivalent of Doctor Dolittle's famed Pushmepullyou, his two-headed llama-type pet. Earlier retirement schemes had been quite flexible, but more bureaucratic arrangements – taxation rules in 1921 stating that 65 was the 'normal' age of retirement; the strong incentive to finish at 65 involved in the 1946 social insurance settlement – made for more uniformity. Other measures pressed workers toward retirement. There was the 1977 Job Release Scheme, which gave people just below pensionable age a bridging payment until that age was reached, provided they were replaced by an unemployed person; and there were the 1981 and 1983 plans, whereby men over 60 and out of work for more than a year might be removed from the unemployment register in exchange for the higher rate of long-term income support. This effectively erased 200,000 men from the unemployment rolls.

There is no doubt that larger firms and many trade unions prefer the straightforward convenience of the sharp cut-off point, and most of the occupational pension schemes also make a virtue of leaving work at what is deemed the proper age. As early as 1977, 53 per cent of retirees had done so because it was mandatory. Nonetheless, commentators still muse over which head of the retirement Pushmepullyou beast rules, and whether men and women are forced into or can't wait for retirement. Perhaps the sort of cultural pressure described in Chapter 3 is at work. Whatever the practical mix of conditions, there is little doubt that it has become a normally accepted piece of 'age-appropriate behaviour' to retire at 60 or 65 (Johnson and Falkingham 1992).[2]

Next it is salutary to remark that official unemployment in the older ranges is much the same as elsewhere, averaging about 8 per cent in the early 1990s. This of course relates to those seeking work and on unemployment benefit; since 1983 unemployed men over 60 have been offered longer-term income support and pensions' credits, and have vanished from the unemployment statistics as such. If one takes a measure of those seeking work rather than on unemployment benefit, one finds a male unemployment rate for the 55–64 age-group rising as high as 18 per cent in 1992. It is perhaps otiose to add that much older age unemployment is of lengthy duration, with, for example, a quarter of all unemployed men and women aged 50–59 having been workless for over three years. For many it is really the beginning of retirement, and doubtless many men and women abandon the attempt and drop forever out of the labour mart.

Sadly, ill-health and disability play a role, accounting, for instance, for no less than half those who take early retirement. Research suggests that this is coloured in several ways, including maybe the deleterious and demoralizing effects of difficult labour conditions, but, perhaps more importantly, the willingness of both employees and medical staff to accept or enforce standards of invalidity or unfitness more readily. There is certainly no general tendency toward poorer health in older age, rather the reverse.

Lastly, there is little chance of these circumstances altering much, even if it were desirable and shelving, for the moment, any discussion of whether the post-work phase is for good or ill. Many commentators believe that the economic malaise of the last quarter century is more or less permanent and that its new reality is here to stay. The same period saw the working population expanded by 2.6 million, which, together with a million extra women eager to enter the workplace, contributed to underemployment. Jobs were increased by two million, it is true, but that left a large shortfall, and a great proportion of these new jobs were part-time and/or self-employed, often casual. It is true that the increase in the working age population is proving to be less during the 1990s than previous two decades, with about half a million workers as the best available estimate, but, over against that, one counts a further addition – roughly three-quarters of a million – to the number of women seeking work.

The very latest preliminary figures, those for 1994, confirm these more detailed findings. In brief, it would seem that, in 1994, only 74 per cent of men aged 55–59 and 50 per cent aged 60–64 had been economically active, and that, taking the two groups together, 37 per cent of men with up to 10 years' working life left had given up the idea of finding employment. The trend of more women working appears to be continuing with, in 1994, 60 per cent of unmarried and 46 per cent of married women economically active, that is either in work or, if unemployed, actively having sought a job in the previous four weeks and prepared to start such a job in the next fortnight. That two-part definition is a meaningful one, for it indicates the resignation of many men as they face the bleak prospects of employment. The social and cultural atmosphere generated suggests that, on the one hand, nearly four out of 10 men of later working age have abandoned hope of finding employment, and, on the other hand, that the concept of early retirement continues to be regarded as socially acceptable.

All in all, it is estimated that there will be a further reduction in older age employment by the end of the century, probably in the scale of another half million, the slight majority of them men. Although many early retirees would like to work – half of unemployed men aged 55–59; a quarter of those 60–64, and even an eighth of those aged 65–69 were so desirous (although several felt they were unceremoniously thrust out of work, with 14 per cent of men and 9 per cent of women among those retiring early) – and although there have been some well-publicized signals of older workers finding jobs, not least in retail distribution, the future is set fair or foul, according to predilection. That is to say, like it or not, large-scale and often early retirement is likely to be the norm over the coming decades, certainly until well into the twenty-first century.

It is but cold comfort to observe that other developed nations have experienced similar trends. Like the United Kingdom, many had high numbers of post-65 workers – in general, around 70 per cent of the age-group – early in the century, falling to 20 or 25 per cent by the 1970s, followed by substantial declines, especially among men in the 60–65 age range, since that time. For example, in Germany there has been a drop from 60 to 32 per cent of 60–65-year-olds working, although the German economy, over this period, managed to retain brisker rates of growth and employment than several of its competitors. The United States has figures rather like the British, down to 79 per cent of the 50–59 and 54 per cent of 60–64 male echelons in employment. Relatively early retirement and comparatively little work in older age must be accepted as normal practice.

The lonely household

Although not strictly aligned to retirement in the occupational sense, a comment on social retirement, that is, from parenting, may be in season. Entry into the third age, as we have noted, is marked by either economic retirement and/or the completion of main-line family roles. There is the emblem of the empty nest as well as the gold clock. Here too we discover that the second age phase of childcare is accomplished earlier, mainly because of a decline in the number of children, on average, reared. In 1900, the average number of children in a family was about three, and the mean age of their mothers when the last child reached 15, that is, on the verge of adulthood, was 50. In the current generation an average of under two is the norm, with the mean age at which the last child becomes 15 having dropped to 45. Since World War II the tendency has been for mothers in the younger age-groups to have most babies; in 1941 17 per cent of live births were to women over 35, but in 1981 that figure had dropped to 6 per cent. Since 1981 women under 25 have had proportionately fewer babies, but that has scarcely affected post-35 births because of what might unsentimentally be called bunching in the 25–35 year range. The record of Moulay Ishmael the Bloodthirsty, who fathered over a thousand children, is unlikely to be challenged in these conditions.

Although because of school and college courses children tumble out of the nest later than they did in 1900, the great majority of children have reached years of discretion and independence – at least, theoretically, one quickly adds for the benefit of the sceptical and anxious parent – when mothers and fathers are in their late 40s or early 50s, if anything, somewhat earlier than the rough indicator of 55 often used for third age statistical purposes. It is true that there are more second families than there used to be, but that does not significantly alter the pattern. The number of births to women over 40, which would mean these children reached 15 when their mothers were 55, is negligible, compared with 5 per cent in 1941. In brief, parents, as well as workers, are dispatching their second age duties more summarily than of yore.

While discussing these family matters, it is important, especially from the viewpoint of the domestic economy of older people, to scrutinize the shape of older households, for there have been many changes in this sphere. Seventy-four per cent of men over 65 are married (leaving 17 per cent single, 6 per cent widowered and 3 per cent divorced or separated) as opposed to as few as 37 per cent of women (10 per cent single, as many as 50 per cent widowed, and 3 per cent divorced or separated). Given the relatively high survival rates of women, this fact is a contributory factor to the number of older people living alone. There are others. Although the passage of time means that this feature is vanishing, the ravages of World War I and the surge of mainly male emigration to the dominions which followed it, led to a wholesale rise in the number of 'never-weds'. A more modern issue is divorce and separation, at one time negligible, but now having risen to its current rate of 3 per cent, with an estimate of 17 per cent in the future.

Then there is the question of children. Although the post-1945 boom in marriage and babies will shortly create another bump in the graph, in 1978 a third of women over 75 had had no children, and a downside to extreme old age is the sad and increasing hazard of outliving one's children. There are good signs as well. The idyll of family life has been overplayed, and many older people are only too pleased to live independently – research by Thompson and West in 1984 revealed that old people regarding moving in with relatives as being as ghastly as entering an institution. Relatives, too, have changed social expectations of where and how they care for their elder relations. They may be less likely to welcome them into their actual home – and of course increased dispersal of families for career and allied reasons may have made that more difficult – as opposed to providing succour in other ways. The motor car and the telephone, for instance, have eased communications, and 90 per cent of third age people report that they have family or friends living 'reasonably' near to them.

The upshot is a rising number of older people who live alone. In the

Table 4.5   Amount of men and women over 55 who are not economically active

Age	Men		Women	
55–59	17%	245,000	50%	739,000
60–64	46%	637,000	80%	1,191,000
65+	92%	3,333,000	96%	5,198,000
		4,215,000		**7,128,000**
Total			**11,343,000**	

Source: Midwinter 1991a

seventeenth century about 10 per cent of the older population lived alone (6 per cent of the older male and 14 per cent of the older female population) and in 1901 it was still exactly 10 per cent (7 per cent male and 13 per cent female, a very similar finding). In 1951 it had shifted a little to 13 per cent (8 per cent male; 16 per cent female) but by 1985 it had leapt to 36 per cent (23 per cent of the male and no less than 47 per cent of the older female age-groups). That is a most compelling statistic. It amounts to just on a third or four million older people living alone, 3.3. million (80 per cent) of them being women. Predictably, 44 per cent of these women are over 75, rising to over a half of those over 80.

The two factors – fewer children bred over a briefer span of time and the increased independent living of older people – have combined to shorten the duration of the nuclear family. For instance, in 1851 20 per cent of households were intergenerational, that is, they included relatives such as grandparents. A hundred years later in 1951 the figure was still as high as 15 per cent. Twenty years later in 1971 it had halved to 7.7 per cent of households, and that decline continues. Indeed, older people are not alone in living alone; a fifth of British housing units are of single occupancy, and there are about as many in the under-25 group – some 25 per cent – as in the 65–69 bracket who are living alone. Where in 1961 one in eight people lived alone, it is now under one in four, and the number of households with five or more people therein has dropped from 14 to 7 per cent in the same time. Only 4 per cent of pensioners live in the same house as a child. It is an age of privacy (Johnson and Falkingham 1992).

The long goodbye

The key point is the length of such retirement. It is here that the two major factors of longer survival and earlier retirement join to create a third age, for many, of new and unprecedented proportions. Taking 55 as a fairly cautious indicator, and bearing in mind those few comments about the familial role, we may hazard the estimate shown in Table 4.5.

Those 11.3 million people, as of 1991, represented 76 per cent or three-quarters of the 14.8 million aged over 55 in the United Kingdom. Given the trends, both in demography and in retirement from employment, it would not be unjust to deploy as a rule of thumb a figure such as 12 million out of 15 million over 55 as we approach the millennium. It is right to recall that a fraction are still working. The over-55s make up one in seven of the men and one in 10 of the women in employment, and that amount – 3.5 million – is not a small proportion. What it also does is to remind us of the more satisfactory usage of 'stage' rather than 'age'; the 70-plus workers have more in social common with their fellow-tillers in the field, with whom they form the second age, than with the retired 50-plus group who help constitute the third age. Moreover, only 8 per cent of men over 65 are working, that is, 289,000, compared with 1939 when 33 per cent of men over 65 were still employed, that is, 778,000.

The 12 million or so retired or third agers are roughly the same number as the under-16 population (11.7 million in 1991; estimated 12.6 million in 2001; and 12 million in 2011). They constitute a good fifth of the whole population and a good quarter of the adult population. These are impressive fractions.

What is more, people occupy the third age or retirement berth for exceptionally long periods. As late as the 1980s government documents could refer, without causing mirth, to retirement as a 'contingency', almost as if it were an emergency which, like the onset of measles, might afflict the careless if they didn't take precautions. Retirement is a racing certainty. There have been dreadful failures of social policy because the salient nature of retirement had not been acknowledged. In truth, apart from the admittedly central monetary consideration of the pension, retirement policy, as such, has been piecemeal. As we have seen, it has been a function of the economy to discard labour as and when it is necessary, so that retirement policy, at best, has been *post hoc*.

Suddenly there are men and women who are in retirement as long as they were in employment and childrearing. The encroachment of education at one end and retirement at the other (and ignoring, for the nonce, the likely interludes of unemployment) could result in people beginning work in their early 20s and finishing in their early 50s, a matter of some 30 or so years in employ. Survival until 85 clearly equals this. Take the lively example of the 8000 centenarians now living in the United Kingdom (as compared, incidentally, to the 250 of 1951), nine out of ten of whom are women. Visualize the case of the person who finishes work and parenting in his or her mid-50s and survives to 100 – such a person would have lived almost as long in retirement as not. As Dick Deadeye, the cynical and twisted sailor of the crew of *HMS Pinafore*, might have observed, 'Aye, it's a queer world'.

Notes

1 This section relies heavily upon the research presented in Trinder *et al.* (1992).
2 Johnson and Falkingham (1992) is an excellent primer on many of these issues.

5

Income maintenance in retirement today

The changeless position

Eventually we reach the nub of the issue: some 12 million people in the United Kingdom locked into a retirement, which for many is of lengthy duration, and in a social context where work is still regarded as the central, almost exclusive, indicator of worth. The question of how and to what degree this quarter of the adult population is or should be financed, a social policy query never before raised at this level of engagement in the story of humankind, is absolutely critical. As we have already observed, it is the crucial arc in a circle of perception and treatment of older age in our society. In the following chapter, the parameters both institutional – the supports and services in kind – and cultural – the influences affecting the decisions taken about both income and services – will be addressed, and the findings of Chapter 3 updated. This chapter, meanwhile, provides an analysis of the income and expenditure of people in the third age in Britain today.

The general position is, perhaps depressingly, very similar to that outlined in Chapter 2. There are still basically two ways of income provision. There is the relatively low, some would say reduced, state pension, scarcely reconsidered as to its root value since its establishment in 1908, with, as throughout the history of welfare provision, means-tested additions for those in particular distress. There is the occupational pension, the chief variation from hitherto being the great increase in the number subscribed to and enjoyed, and with legislation passed enabling the state to be a player in the work-related pensions game.

Two other introductory points might be made. As in the past, the more well-to-do people have made self-provision through personal savings, investments and pension schemes, but in the broadest sense such plans are the close cousins of occupational pensions, in that ordinarily they arise from income originating in or from the workplace. These more well-to-do people have always benefited from owning and inheriting property, finding therein a ready succour in old age. There is evidence that this has been enhanced by the huge switch over the past two or three generations from the private rental to the owner-occupation of domestic properties. This has brought the chance of extra relief in older age to many more people, and has, of course, resulted in many children (often on the verge of third age themselves) inheriting such estates from their even more elderly parents. What's more, it is evident that owner-occupation has usually been the product of people repaying mortgages out of salaries, so that, once more, if indirectly, the income from this practice is work-related.

Indeed, work remains central to the whole pattern of income maintenance in older age. It is safe to state that the United Kingdom has never had a retirement policy declared as such. There has been a bundle of attitudes, even prejudices, but these have been made manifest not in a retirement policy *per se*, but in a *pensions* policy. This dictates much of when retirements occur and what shape they take; the money comes first. It is perhaps fairer to suggest that, having agreed that 60 or 65 is the correct age to give up work, the fixing of pensions at and around those points ensures that this view of retirement is endorsed.

The post-war settlement

We must first bring matters up to date from where we left them, roughly at the outbreak of World War II, in Chapter 2. The Beveridge Report, *Social Insurance and Allied Services*, published amidst acclaim in 1942, offered a blueprint for a modern welfare state, and its widespread adoption was the nearest the British had come to a wholesale national revision since the Poor Law Amendment Act of 1834. Moreover, no government has since risked so basic a reformulation.

It is true that several of the precepts of the emergent welfare state amounted to a tidying up and an enlargement of existing practice, but the outcome was a regular and coherent view of welfare provision. The crux lay in its universalism, its acceptance that welfare was not so much a matter of doling out the equivalent of alms to those in distress, but an issue which embraced all. It had civic virtue at its core, with an underlying message that all should give that all might benefit, and that collective provision was mightier, morally and practically, than self-help. It was welcomed in a mood of common citizenship engendered by the war experience, whereby effective and rational planning in the public interest had been seen to be good.

Sir William Beveridge identified several categories of distress, including retirement. They were to be relieved by flat-rate benefits, funded by revenue from the flat-rate contributions of employees, employers and the state, but he found it necessary to add – to retain, yet again – a means-tested safety-net for emergency and miscellaneous cases (Beveridge 1942). It must be stressed that his assumption was that there would be perpetual full employment, and that there would be state action to guarantee this condition. Full employment obviated the need for anything but a reactive assistance system of relatively small size, just as it generated the taxation to pay for such welfare provision.

During the 1940s and early 1950s the unemployment rate hardly rose above 1 per cent.

The major statute in fulfilment of these proposals was the 1946 National Insurance Act, which, alongside other legislation, including the National Health Service, came into effect on 5 July 1948. The standard flat-rate benefit was initially 26 shillings (£1.30) a week, whether for illness, unemployment or retirement, with 42 shillings (£2.10) for a retired married couple. The Labour politician Jim Griffiths, who oversaw the creation of this new welfare system, bravely determined to make that pension available to all immediately, as opposed to Beveridge's more wary proposition of a 20-year sliding scale. Thus the pension leapt all at once by 16 shillings (80p), the largest single increase so far in its history, for it had remained stationary since just after the World War I.

It was a generous decision, part of an intrepid commitment to social welfare, which some right-wing economists in hindsight have since lamented, in that it siphoned finance away from industrial revival and renewal. However, the commitment was definitely in tune with the political mood of the era, and in respect of the retirement pension, it must be remembered that, overall, wages had risen substantially during the war and the differential between wage and pension had automatically suffered. All of this was paid for, theoretically, by national insurance contributions from employer and employee, but such was the demand, that Beveridge's strict view of the insurance dimension was destroyed immediately. It became a pay-as-you-go scheme, a form of tax for current expenditure, rather than a direct insurance programme (Barker 1984; Lowe 1993).

In the broadest terms, there the system lay. It is important to note the retention of the subordinate scheme of means-tested benefits – supplementary benefits, as they were named for much of this post-war era – to shore up the pension. Often as many as two million and more pensioners would be in receipt of such subventions, the continuing theme being the inadequacy of the basic income. Of course, especially as inflation took a spiralling grasp in the 1960s and 1970s, the pension was increased in monetary terms, in line with the higher prices or wages, invariably the latter, but without its real value gaining substantially although there were some temporary upward flips in the middle 1970s.

Taking a point of reference in the early and mid-1980s, when the old age pension was £36 and the average industrial wage about £150, the pension was still less than a third of the standard manual worker's wage, and in fact it has never risen above two-fifths of that average income since its inauguration in 1908. Moreover, in the period from the early 1950s to the early 1980s, during which the number of old age pensioners rose, for reasons which have been alluded to, by a quarter, the fraction of the gross national product devoted in overall terms to elderly people remained unchanged at roughly 9 per cent. The inflationary figures and the growing proportion of older people tended to mask the absence of genuine improvement; in the 20 years before 1980, the pension bill sprang from just short of £4 to nearly £11 billion, but there was little real movement in relative conditions (Thomson 1984).

All this was happening in the so-called Butskellite phase of political consensus, that portmanteau title borrowing from the Conservative and

Labour politicians, R.A. Butler and Hugh Gaitskell. Although some commentators are now inclined to think that the Conservatives were more hawk-like in this respect than was then believed, it did appear that, in pursuit of the fully-fledged welfare state, constructed by Clement Attlee's busy Labour administration of 1945–51, there was some kind of bipartisan truce or bargain to manage it without fundamental change. At the same time, there was considerable discussion, much of it engendered by the trade unions, rather envious of the excellent occupational pensions chiefly enjoyed by the professional and managerial classes, about work-related supplements.

There was much hectoring and bickering, and varied plans were submitted, until Harold Wilson's Labour government passed the 1975 Social Security Pensions Act. This established the State Earnings Pension Scheme (SERPS) which came into being in 1978, and which at maximum offered a supplement of 25 per cent of final earnings and an accrual period of 20 years of employment. Those who were already in existing schemes could contract out of SERPS. It was perhaps a natural development of a society enjoying full employment, and in historical terms, it was of huge import. For the first time, the twin roads of the subsistence pension and the occupational pension came close to convergence, as the state determined to be the builder of both (Johnson and Falkingham 1992).

The post-war settlement unsettled

Full employment paid for and encouraged the development of both state and occupational pensions, and their eventual combination in SERPS. The decline of full employment after the late 1970s had the reverse effect.

It may be some years before historians are able to assess the degree of blame that should be attached to politics or to economics for this deterioration. In most countries, after World War II, a collective or interventionist ethic had reigned, with welfare services and full employment more or less in harmony. The extreme case was perhaps to be found in the state capitalist phalanx of East European nations, the so-called communist bloc, but the United States, Japan and the then West Germany had adopted policies facing in the same direction. The last quarter of the twentieth century has witnessed a change in both political and economic outlook. Free marketing, private enterprise and monetarist approaches have replaced the post-war convention of largely state-managed economies, whilst the global economy has grown more starkly competitive and meaner. Again, the extreme case is represented by the freeing of the East European nations, including the Russian republics, from heavy state controls, with, at whatever profit in increased liberty, a huge extension of unemployment.

That brief excursion into global happenings was intended to show that the United Kingdom was not alone in having experienced the joint rigours of economic dislocation and right-wing governance, associated chiefly with the premiership of Margaret Thatcher (1979–90). Right-wing critics of Mrs Thatcher's ilk were able to argue that 'irresponsible' Keynesian policies were to blame for economic laxity, with increasing money supply for welfare and allied amenities leading to hefty inflation and bulging budgets. The call for tighter monetary controls and a return to the purity of the market also came in response to anxieties about the downside of welfarism. It was argued that welfare politics, far from having eradicated poverty, had fashioned a veritable 'serfdom' of dependent folk, their sinews of enterprise deadened by the 'treacle-well' state.

In whatever mix, this compound of world economic ravages and neo-liberal politics undermined the construct of full employment, in that men and women found themselves either out of work or in much less stable working circumstances. The effects were twofold. We have already traced in Chapter 4 how late unemployment merged with early retirement to extract people from out of the workforce, and these were but a fraction of the thousands – it occasionally touched three million during this period and unofficial estimates were rather higher – who were unemployed, awaiting training or had removed themselves from the workforce. Beveridge had predicated his comprehensive scheme on the notion that the only unemployed would be those not able to work, not those not wanted for work, and the new dispensation ruined this overnight. The very people who should have been paying the taxes and national insurance contributions to maintain the welfare system were in dire need of benefits themselves.

In a sense, society had two unemployment problems, blurring at the fringes. One was the second age group of unemployed and underemployed people, and the other the third age group, formed by good – increased survival – and ill – unwanted early release from work – methods. Neither had been foreseen. Both drew heavily on the public coffers. By the mid-1990s, in rounded terms, some £93 billion was being expended on benefits (£86 billion) and welfare (£7 billion) in the United Kingdom. Together this amounted, in real values, to eight times as much as was paid out in the 1940s, when the ground was laid for the post-war welfare settlement. It compared with £29 billion on education and £37 billion on the National Health Service and amounted to 16 per cent of the gross national product of £581 billion.

Some £10 billion went on direct unemployment benefits, with an estimated £2 or £3 billion in additional social security payments to those wholly or partially unemployed; it was estimated that an unemployed person cost the state £9000 a year. Some £29 billion were now spent on the contributory state pension (£27 billion for the basic pension, £2 billion for the earnings-related element), with the non-contributory pensions and the Christmas bonus costing just £170 million, and with, once more, some central and local monies additionally to top this up, by way, for example, of housing benefit. No less than three million pensioners (including some 1.7 million over-60s on income support, the replacement of supplementary benefit as the chief topping-up scheme) required help from such means-tested benefits to eke out the rather austere basic pension. Indeed the overall numbers of social beneficiaries requiring the age-old safety-net had risen overall from 10 per cent in the late 1940s to 30 per cent in the mid-1990s. With a large slice of the £20 billion spent on sickness and disability benefits and the £2 billion spent on widows' pensions plainly going to older people, it was estimated that the sum total of welfare payments to the elderly in 1994–95 were £38 billion, two-fifths of the overall budget. There was, of course, revenue. The national insurance fund grossed

£45 billion in 1992, £34 billion in contributions, and the rest in investment income, out of which £41 billion was expended, a useful present to the exchequer (Johnson and Falkingham 1992).

A government elected to lower taxes and public expenditure as part of its programme of lifting state shackles and letting loose market forces had been determined to face up to this dilemma. The central plank in the Conservative administration's reworking of welfare legislation was the 1986 Social Security Act, which affected older people in several ways. SERPS came in for criticism, with the government alarmed by the rising figures involved. This 1976–78 resolution, which it had been hoped would command cross-party support over a lengthy period, was thus revised after only a few years, although steps to dismantle it altogether were avoided. By reducing the full pension from a quarter to a fifth (the consequence of making the career-spread average, not the best years, the measure) and by halving the widow's allowance, it was estimated that this earnings-related scheme would lower the mid-twenty-first century outlay from £35 to £16 billion.

Of more immediate worry, an early reform of the Thatcher ministry had been the decision to make the weekly pension price-oriented, rather than related to whichever of earnings or prices was the higher in the given year, a none too subtle method of reducing its growth. By 1993, it was calculated that a retired married couple might be losing as much as £25 a week as a result. It is fair to point out that the earnings rule, whereby state pensioners lost benefit against any such earnings, was abolished in 1989, a move welcomed by the not negligible minority of post-65 workers, but a move which made no measurable difference to retirement as such or to the overall situation of pensioners. In 1993 it was resolved, under European pressure, to equalize the male and female criteria, to raise the women's state pension threshold to 65, rather than, on grounds of cost, lower the men's to 60. It may be recalled that, because of the difficulties older women had then experienced in finding work, their age eligibility had been reduced to 60 in 1940.

It was calculated, with melodramatic bravura, that the state pension, worth 17 per cent of the average male manual worker's wage in 1908, 19 per cent in 1948, and having advanced to but 22 per cent by 1985, decreased to 16 per cent in 1990, that is, below the original 1908 figure. Moreover, it was claimed that, if the price index continued to be utilized and if earnings rose at an average of 1.5 per cent a year, the value of the pension, apropos the male manual employee's wage, would be a scanty 7 per cent by early in the next century. These reductions continued to underscore the patently evident fact that the Beveridge 'insurance' proposals had been intended to provide contingency relief. As provision for long periods of financial distress, they were seen to be insufficient and in no manner identifiable with a living wage.

On the other hand, and in logical keeping with its notion of 'privatism', the Conservative government was keen to encourage occupational or individual pensions, and there was appropriate legislation. Portability of pensions with a career move, the lack of which had certainly been a bugbear for ambitious job-seekers, and wider choice for employees were implemented. The forays on SERPS and the temptations strewn before the potential private pension-holder led to five million people opting out of SERPS by 1994. It has been suggested

Table 5.1   Occupational pension involvement as a percentage of those employed

Year	Male		Female		All	
1956	6.4m	43%	1.6m	21%	8.0m	35%
1975	8.6m	63%	2.8m	30%	11.4m	49%
1987	7.2m	60%	3.4m	35%	10.6m	49%

Source: Johnson and Falkingham 1992

that at least two million of this number have chosen a pension scheme which, because of the low level of their earnings, will be less than the state alternative they have eschewed, while 450,000 others left existing occupational plans with a guaranteed outcome related to final salary, for much less secure private pension schemes. Significantly, generous tax relief was offered, amounting to a cost on the exchequer of close on £14 billion annually by the 1990s. This was about half the cost of the state pension, and should be properly acknowledged as a further spending on older age, on that base making this total expenditure something close to £52 billion.

The number of all adults, at work or unemployed, who were in pension schemes had stayed constant at about 50 per cent for many years. It rose quickly to 65 per cent during the Thatcher years, with signs of further augmentation. By 1990 over 11 million employees were involved in occupational and personal pension plans, and already over four million (more than two-fifths of state pensioners, something like double the 1970 figure) were receiving the just deserts of such schemes, although some of these were minute in amount. Occupational pensions still remained largely the province of the middle classes. At this juncture, only a third of waged workers, against three-quarters of salaried employees, were in private schemes, and only a quarter of council house and private let tenants, as opposed to three-quarters of owner-occupiers. The advance of the occupational pension may be exemplified in Table 5.1.

Two comments: the pre-war (1936) amount was only 13 per cent; and the consistency of the overall 49 per cent hides an interesting male fall-back and female rush-forward. Moreover, the numbers involved in occupational pension schemes continue to rise. Later figures, as of 1992, show that 62 per cent of full-time male, 55 per cent of full-time female and 19 per cent of part-time female workers are in employers' pension schemes, and that 27 per cent full-time male, 21 per cent of full-time female and 12 per cent of part-time female workers have joined personal pension plans.

A fascinating cultural sidelight was offered by the rumpus during the mid-1990s about the inefficient, some alleged, criminally self-interested, advice given by parts of the private market to would-be personal occupational pensioners. This was in contra-distinction to the derogatorily-termed 'nanny' state, which rather anonymously and unimaginatively had tried to manage people's pension arrangements in the Butskellite era. In the bracing freshness of the market, each individual was expected to watch out for his or her own financial back, and the argument about whether the ordinary person was automatically resilient or vulnerable was widely heard in the land. The Goode Committee Report of 1993 was an attempt to bring some order to this troubled scene (Savage *et al*. 1994).

Income in old age[1]

With the end of the twentieth century nigh, the retirement situation in the United Kingdom might be summarized thus: there are approaching 12 million people in the third age, the vast majority of them enjoying pensionable income, either directly or via a spouse, including some 10 million on the state pension, approaching six million requiring means-tested benefits, and over four million with occupational pensions. It is time to examine what all these incomes amount to in terms of the day by day life of the individuals concerned.

Looked at in the global sense, there had been some argument whether pensioner incomes had deteriorated over the years. One school of thought, highly vocal in the United States, viewed the stage of the 1970s and 1980s cynically as a glittering one for old people, upon which they continued to complain loudly about their miserly pittance. Official and academic sources argued in the United Kingdom that pensioner incomes had grown twice as fast as the income of the population as a whole between 1951 and 1986, and that their disposable income per head was now 70 per cent of the non-pensioner average income, as compared with 40 per cent at the earlier date.

This surprising finding that the average income of older people had grown in real terms by about a third was hotly contested. The extremely low base from which the rise had occurred was called in evidence, as were the 2.3 million and more pensioners who in 1987, by dint of receiving less than 50 per cent of the average income, were officially deemed to dwell in poverty. It appeared that the result was more favourable if the arithmeticians stressed personal rather than household income. The rise in female employment from 35 per cent in 1951 to 49 per cent in 1986, with a subsequent increase in two-salaried families, coupled with a drop in the average size of the non-pensioner household from 3.6 to 2.7 over the same period, has tended to raise the level of income pouring into such households, whereas the pensioner household is more heavily reliant on the direct input of usually one pension only. Viewed in that light, it seemed that older people enjoyed a better standard of living in the 1950s, relative to the population at large, than they did in the 1980s (Fiegehen 1986; Hutton 1994).

It is also instructive to examine how the constituents of pensioner incomes have changed over roughly that same post-war period, as shown in Table 5.2. In brief, there has been a definite swap, as might be expected, between employment and pension as chief contributors. Despite the great increase in occupational pensioners, the rise in percentage is not as high as one might have thought. In 1953 barely 900,000 were in receipt of occupational and allied pensions, whereas by 1987 that figure had jumped to over four million, as we have noted, to which must be added 1.3 million widows, benefiting as surviving dependants.

Table 5.2   Constituents of pensioner incomes, 1951 and 1986

Percentage of pensioner age income	1951	1986
All social security etc.	43	59
Occupational pensions	15	20
Savings	15	14
Employment	27	7

Source: Johnson and Falkingham 1992

Table 5.3   Weekly income of bottom and top decile pensioners, 1987

Pensioner income (£)	Bottom decile	Top decile
All social security etc.	42.80	64.50
Occupational pensions	1.66	78.40
Savings	2.70	78.60
Employment	0.20	33.30
Total	**47.36**	**254.80**

Source: Johnson and Falkingham 1992

Let us transform those elements into real money, using 1987 as a basis, and comparing the bottom with the top decile or tenth of pensioners, assessed by income (Table 5.3.). The most notable characteristic of the two sets of figures is that the state directly contributes 90 per cent of the one and only 25 per cent of the other. One might have predicted the vastly improved chances of savings and occupational pensions; indeed, only 23 per cent of the bottom decile have occupational pensions, and rather tiny ones by the look of the figures, against 81 per cent of the highest decile. But even state pensions, in part the consequence of abandoning flat-rate for earnings-related benefits, and also employment chances are much better among the upper tenth.

The changes in housing stock should also be recalled. Older households still lagged behind the mainstream in 1990, in that only 52 per cent were owner-occupiers (64 per cent all housing units) with 39 per cent who were local authority tenants (30 per cent all housing units) and 9 per cent who were in privately rented or housing association property (only 6 per cent all housing units). This, of course, is a generation rather than an age effect, with the situation changing rapidly; even by 1993 the continuing effect of the government's council house sales and other housing policies had again reduced the number of council tenants and increased the number of private let and allied tenants, although the general effect on pensioners, as from 1990, was still not very pronounced. It should also be remembered that, unlike the younger generation, all but about 4 or 5 per cent of the older breed are geniune owner-occupiers, no longer owing a huge mortgage to their building society. The valuation of the housing stock thus held by older people is put at £218

Table 5.4   Median and average weekly pensioner income (in pounds), 1989

Pensioner income	Median	Average	Percentage in receipt
All social security etc.	62	71	97 (i.e. 3% no state aid)
Occupational pensions	5	37	52 (i.e. 48% no occupational pension)
Savings	2	24	65 (i.e. 35% no savings)
Earnings	0	24	13 (i.e. 87% no earnings)
Total	**69**	**156**	

Source: Hancock and Weir 1994

billion (1990 figures) with an estimate that by the end of the century that value will be £279 billion.

It must, however, be pointed out that the houses of older people tend to be less valuable and less well-maintained than the norm, and that there is something of a myth surrounding the notion of 'income poor/house rich' pensioners who should be able to provide out of this bounty for personal needs; 'income rich/house rich' is nearer the truth. The fallout from this massive holding – already it is beginning to be inherited by putative and actual 'young' third agers to swell their estates; already it is being deployed to pay for the health care of its debilitated, ageing owners – will be discussed later and in Chapter 6.

Another angle on pensioner income is to scrutinize the median figures, that is to say the income level below and above which precisely half the pensioner cohort exists, studied as unit, that is, household, income proceeds. In the 10 years from 1979 to 1989 this figure rose from £72 per week (67 per cent of median non-pensioner income of £108) to £83 per week (62 per cent of £134), a rise of 15 per cent (24 per cent non-pensioner equivalent). That masks a definite widening of the gap between top and bottom. The median for the top decile was, in 1979, three times that of the bottom decile; in 1989, it was four and a half times as much. Where the top tenth median had shot up by 50 per cent, the bottom tenth median had struggled up a sparse 7.5 per cent (Hancock and Weir 1994).

Occupational pensions and the diminishing value of the state pension accounted for a good deal of this. Using the same decade, the median income in 1979 for the non-occupational pensioner was £69 per week and for the occupational pensioner (44 per cent of the whole pensioner group) it was £78, a difference of £9 or 13 per cent. Ten years later in 1989 the respective figures were, for the non-occupational pensioner, £63 – the participation rate in occupational pensions, now at 55 per cent, had actually pushed down that income – and for the occupational pensioner £98, a difference of £35 or 56 per cent. That is a telling effect.

It is an effect which very much influences the vast differential between that median income of £69 per week in 1989, and the average income, which was as high as £156, a vivid demonstration of how comparatively few enjoy the delights of a goodish income, as the analysis in Table 5.4 further explains.

Table 5.5   Gross pensioner income in single and double households, 1993

Gross income (£)	All	Single household	Double household
All social security	91	77	112
Occupational pensions	42	26	69
Savings	27	19	41
Earnings etc.	10	6	17
Total	**170**	**128**	**239**

Source: Government Statistical Service 1995

Median earnings were so small as scarcely to register, while, of the £5 indicated for median private pensions only £2 was, in fact, gleaned from occupational schemes, in contrast to £33 out of £37 for the average pensioner income. The state ingredient is strong in both sets of figures: private pensions, savings and earnings account for the difference in kind rather than degree.

For a fuller description of these differences, it is possible to consider the contrasting cases of where there is a single pensioner and a double pensioner household, of some import in a world where there are 'married couples'' pensions and the like. In 1989 the mean or average weekly income for a single pensioner household was £105 and for a two-person unit £208, whilst the corresponding sums at the median mark were £72 and £149, again significant differences. Updating that a little to 1993, we might proffer the summary shown in Table 5.5.

Moreover, by 1995, 2.6 million of the 6.6 million women pensioners were enjoying the proceeds of their own insurance contributions as a weekly average of £58 (all women pensioners, £53), leaving 2.1 million women reliant on their husbands' contributions to national insurance. This realized an average weekly income of £36, against the men's weekly average state pension of £73, whereas 1.9 million widows were in receipt of a weekly average of £64. On these figures, the all-round average for state income was £60, as we have seen, barely 19 per cent of average earnings. These statistics include additional pensions (that is, SERPS), attendance allowances, invalidity benefits and so forth. In fact, 182,000 retirement pensioners were receiving attendance allowances and invalidity additions to their pensions, while 4.2 million (2.5 million men and 1.7 million women) were already in receipt of additional pensions, but the weekly average income from these was as little as £9.

A word about the non-contributory pensioners, those who were over pensionable age in 1948: these now comprise a tiny number, just 28,000, of whom only 6000 are men. A minute addition is made to the pensions of those over 80. There are also 100,000 state pensioners who themselves have dependants: 84,000 of these cases concern an adult, in 8000 cases it is a child, and in the other 8000 cases it is both an adult and a child. Since the 1986 Social Security Act, the principal form of supplementary benefit became known as income support. This was paid out during 1993 to well over 5 million people, of whom 1.7 million were over 60, including 1.4 million already on a state pension. The average benefit was £55 per week, with the 60-plus echelon getting an average of £44 (pensioners, £38; non-pensioners, £76).

All in all, the figures disguise a very broad array of incomes, with the hefty sums enjoyed by relatively few pensioners at the richer end of that gamut distorting the balance. Although the statistic was lower than the 79 per cent of 1979, 63 per cent of pensioners were dependent for 75 per cent or more of their income on the basic pension, and were in need of forms of means-tested supplements. Pension and benefits together, the state contributed 86 per cent or more to the income of a half of the single and 68 per cent or more to a half of the double pensioner households.

In 1991, although the occupational pension schemes were obviously flourishing, there were still over 40 per cent of pensioners who had no such help, and the occupational pensions being paid were very diverse in value. The average occupational pension was by 1995 £74 per week (£54 for a single and £95 for a double pensioner household), and for those who had savings revenue from investments, the weekly figure averaged £37. Nonetheless, occupational and other forms of private pension contribute less than 4 per cent to the income of a half of pensioners, and savings less than 2 per cent. It is difficult to ignore the conclusion of several commentators that the occupational pension provides an addition or supplement to, rather than an alternative to, the state pension. It is worth bearing this in mind at a time when the case is urged for possibly abandoning the state scheme in favour of a comprehensive occupational pension approach (Hancock and Weir 1994).

Expenditure in old age[2]

Eventually it is what people spend, rather than what they earn, which constitutes some measure of their quality of life. This examination is undertaken by household rather than by individual, in the belief that this offers the more effective means of rational comparison. So many purchases and expenses are collective, not least the ever knotty problem of expenditure on housing itself. Naturally, there is scope for much personal spending within the household accounts, although, in practice, individual records often tell more about who does the shopping or who pays the bills, rather than who does the consuming – women on state pensions spend, on average, twice as much as men, but they do not gobble double what their menfolk eat. In any event, the huge majority of pensioner households are composed of one or two people, a matter remarked on previously, so that less is lost in the analysis, compared, for instance, with a family household including young children.

Moreover, the most up-to-date statistics from the 1994 *General Household Survey* (OPCS 1996) suggest that household size is falling ever more sharply. Where it was close on three persons per household in 1971, it is now down to 2.4 persons per household. Thus the decision to scrutinize one-person and two-person pensioner households in respect of expenditure is not too inapt, even when ranged against all households. Nonetheless, it is true that households including children are obviously faced with particular forms of expenditure, and therefore a more direct comparison will be drawn between pensioner households and non-pensioner households without children. A final reminder is that, although the statistics to be presented relate primarily to official pensioner households, it should not be forgotten that the concept of the third age and the reality of retirement in the United Kingdom require some acknowledgement that many men and women under pensionable age are living in similar circumstances.

First of all, here is a sketch of the way the respective households are divided, using Department of the Environment projections for England and Wales (CSO 1991; OPCS 1992) as the basis (1991 figures). Of the 19 million households in England and Wales, 6.6 million, or 30 per cent, were headed by a person of pensionable age, and these were divided, in rounded numbers, as follows:

Single men	11.5%	650,000 persons
Single women	42.0%	2,350,000 persons
Married couples	37.5%	2,200,000 persons
Other	9.0%	1,500,000 persons

In summary, well over 90 per cent of people of pensionable age live in a one or two-person household, remembering that many of the 'other' households comprise two pensioners who are not married couples, but, for instance, brothers or sisters. Less than 1 per cent of 'older' housing consists of people who are not married, in common-law partnerships, or otherwise related. Of course, not all the married couples are of pensionable age; that figure includes some where the spouse has not yet reached that juncture, although, obviously enough, many will be approaching that point. In fact, only 1 per cent of women over 65 have a husband under 65, although predictably the reverse figure is higher. However these figures take no account of the cases where a non-pensioner is head of the household and a pensioner, most usually a spouse, is also resident.

By the end of the century it is likely that the number of these so-called older households will have risen by 4 per cent or 230,000 actual housing units. Of that total of 6.8 million households in England and Wales, 3.3 million (49 per cent) will be single person dwellings, three-quarters of them the homes of women.

These findings hold steady for the United Kingdom as a whole, and Table 5.6 is designed to show how all pensioners are distributed in terms of household. The relevant percentages for non-pensioner headed households are included for comparative purposes, whilst for ease of reference, the relatively few households headed by a non-pensioner but having a pensioner resident have been embraced among the pensioner clan.

By and large, approaching 7 million of the United Kingdom's 22 million housing units – that is, a third – contain at least one pensioner, and, in approximate proportions, these are comprised of close on 4 million pensioner-only households, over 2 million joint pensioner households, and half a million where pensioners and non-pensioners cohabit. What is apparent is that a comparison of expenditure, utilizing one and two-person households, comprehends the vast majority – indeed, over nine-tenths – of pensioners. As for non-pensioner housing, two-fifths of households where a man is the head, and over a third of those where a woman is the head, are either one or

Table 5.6 Heads of household – pensionable and non-pensionable status: United Kingdom, mid-1990s

Category	Head of household				
	Pensioners			Non-pensioners	
	Men	Women	All	Men	Women
Single	23% 0.8m	47% 3.1m	36% 3.9m	10%	7%
Double	67% 2.3m	47% 3.1m	49% 5.4m	28%	26%
Other	10% 0.4m	6% 0.5m	15% 0.9m	62%	67%
	3.5m	6.7m	10.2m		

Source: Falkingham and Gordon 1990

Table 5.7 Household expenditure in various categories: United Kingdom, 1991

	Average weekly expenditure	
	Mean	Median
Pensioner	£109	£ 85
Non-pensioner	£164	£138
Pensioner, excluding housing	£ 97	£ 74
Non-pensioner, excluding housing	£135	£113

Source: Smeaton and Hancock 1995

two-person households, representing approximately another 5.5 million households or nearly a quarter of the total – thus the argument for a cross-check against non-pensioner households of those sizes also has some validity (Falkingham and Gordon 1990). With this background in mind, it is time to look at the relevant household expenditures.

As a baseline, let us begin with some general statistics about weekly spending. 1991 figures reveal interesting differences between mean and median points, between average pensioner and average non-pensioner, and between, ever a critical area, housing and non-housing considerations (Table 5.7). Figures from 1995 are shown in Tables 5.8 and 5.9.

These numbers confirm the commonsensical notion that, on average, work is more profitable than either retirement or unemployment. Both fall a parlous way behind the norm, even allowing for the fact that family expenditure on children is encompassed by both the 'employed' and 'social class' figures, the latter, of their nature, being based on economic activity. Given the greater

Table 5.8   Average household weekly expenditure according to household head's employment status

Full-time employee	£379
Part-time employee	£245
Self-employed	£402
Unemployed	£176
Unoccupied	£214
Retired	£157
All	£284

Source: Central Statistical Office 1995b

Table 5.9   Average household weekly expenditure according to household head's social class

Social class I	(professional)	£478
Social class II	(intermediate)	£423
Social class IIIN	(skilled non-manual)	£299
Social class IIIM	(skilled manual)	£325
Social class IV	(partly skilled)	£265
Social class V	(unskilled)	£218
Retired		£176

Source: Central Statistical Office 1995b

likelihood of unemployed people having families to cater for, it might be guessed that, on average, they are even worse off than the average pensioner.

So to the core of the matter, with some account of the actual weekly spending of pensioners on the various commodities and services which go to make up the household economy. Six groups have been targeted with this in mind. They are of two kinds – one-person and two-person households – each of three degrees – retired households mainly dependent on state pensions, using the criterion of at least three-quarters of the household income deriving from state sources; retired households not mainly dependent on state pensions and benefits, but where, for instance, private/occupational pensions and savings play a larger role; and non-retired households. In the case of the two-person households, the figures always relate to the 'one man, one woman' format, which is by far the commonest example of the genre, although, naturally enough, there are some instances of pairs of the same gender sharing a household. For ease of reference and comparison, the figures – all of them for the year 1994–95 – have been normally rounded up to the nearest pound.

The first raft of statistics explores the range of spending within each of the six categories, according to gross weekly income. It employs the commonly used device of differentiating between the three essential forms of expenditure, namely, housing, fuel and power, and food and non-alcoholic drink, and the remainder of spending on such diverse items as clothing, household goods, travel and leisure. Ordinarily, the lower the income, the higher the proportion expended on the triple necessities, so much so that some experts believe that if 30 per cent of expenditure or more is devoted to food, then that is a sign of poverty. The information in Table 5.10a – 'one-person state pension' households – relates to actual incomes, for here the range of money involved is very low, from about £60 to £100. The other five tables are addressed by way of quintiles, that is, the lowest or first, second, third, fourth and highest fifth or 20 per cent of the appropriate group in respect of income.

An initial purpose of exhibiting this data in tabular form is to show how wide the gamut of expenditure is, within as well as across the categories. This is particularly noticeable in the 'one-person non-retired' group, with its range of £76 to £333 and an associated low average of £190. This reminds us that poverty is not the sole lot of the poorer pensioner, but a structural flaw in the domestic economy of the nation. That lower point of £76 reflects, in all probability, unemployment and ill-paid work, perhaps especially among the young and among single women.

That should not, of course, deflect complete attention from the fate of the state pensioner households, either of one or two persons, and the higher pointers of £76 and £145 respectively suggest what economic difficulties might be suffered by the many thousands in those groups, certainly when compared with the other four sets. What is quite striking is that the 'essential' element of the two 'state pension' types of household is, as would be expected, high, standing at 53 per cent for the one and 48 per cent for the two-person household, while the proportions in the other two matching pairs are not only lower but quite close – 43 and 37 per cent for the two 'occupational pension' groups and 42 and 36 per cent for the two 'non-retired' types. 'State pensioner' households have only about half their income available after the necessities have been found, whereas all the others have upward of three-fifths of income ready for strictly inessential purchases.

Always bearing in mind these broad ranges of spending, it is worth while examining the specific expenditure, commodity by commodity, of the six average levels of spending which emerged from this scrutiny of retired and non-retired households (Table 5.11, see p. 68). As well as rounding up the poundage of these figures, some allied 'expenditure groups' – for instance, alcoholic drink and tobacco; leisure items; household items – have been joined together as a means of simplifying the presentation of the data.

A word about some of those individual 'expenditure groups'. It has already been agreed that housing, with its mix of rents to pay and mortgages paid, with its differences of value according to social and geographic location, and with its varying demands on maintenance costs, is a troublesome feature for the analyst. In the averages, the usual upward gradient from state pensioner to non-retired person holds, with the higher costs obviously reflecting many mortgage repayments. What is fascinating about fuel and power is the relative similarity of all the figures, with, for instance, single non-retired and state pensioned persons spending about the same. It suggests that a household, rich or poor, with one or two dwellers, takes much the same to heat and light, and that, from a sternly logical view of income, it is a feature where no wide range of funding is necessary.

The cost of food for each pair of one and two-person households rather puts

Table 5.10   Weekly household expenditure by categories: United Kingdom 1994–95

a One-person retired 'state pension' household

Gross weekly income	£ expenditure		
	Essential	Other	Total
Under £65	35	28	63
£65–70	38	33	71
£70–85	40	32	72
£85+	46	49	95
All	40 (53%)	36 (47%)	76

b One-person retired 'occupational pension' household

Gross weekly income Quintile	£ expenditure		
	Essential	Other	Total
First	52	41	93
Second	58	65	123
Third	58	70	128
Fourth	65	98	163
Fifth	72	136	208
All	61 (43%)	82 (57%)	143

c One-person non-retired household

Gross weekly income Quintile	£ expenditure		
	Essential	Other	Total
First	39	37	76
Second	62	65	127
Third	76	114	190
Fourth	91	134	225
Fifth	127	206	333
All	79 (42%)	111 (58%)	190

d Two-person retired 'state pension' household

Gross weekly income Quintile	£ expenditure		
	Essential	Other	Total
First	60	58	118
Second	61	65	126
Third	68	61	129
Fourth	73	86	159
Fifth	80	111	191
All	68 (47%)	77 (53%)	145

e Two-person retired 'occupational pension' household

Gross weekly income Quintile	£ expenditure		
	Essential	Other	Total
First	71	88	159
Second	95	95	190
Third	83	122	205
Fourth	93	184	277
Fifth	109	245	354
All	88 (37%)	149 (63%)	237

f Two-person non-retired household

Gross weekly income Quintile	£ expenditure		
	Essential	Other	Total
First	84	115	199
Second	109	174	283
Third	119	193	312
Fourth	138	246	384
Fifth	174	369	543
All	124 (36%)	220 (64%)	344

Source: Central Statistical Office 1995b

the lie to the old adage that two may live as cheaply as one. The two-person household in each pairing comes remarkably close to exactly doubling the one-person costing. Leisure goods and services constitute another example where spending is of that order, with twice as much being spent by the double as by the single household. Housing, unsurprisingly and importantly, is the only piece of expenditure where the one-person/two-person ratio is not high, but most of the other items show extra expenditure, some of it substantial. Motoring is a very clear illustration of where the difference is very considerable, with the two-person household expending comparatively big sums of money. In a regime where dual living is scarcely advantageous, where, for example, the married couple's state pension is a long way from being twice the size of the single person's pension, this issue is well worthy of remark.

However, that is hardly as significant as the great chasm which opens up between the richer and the poorer in older age. Those we have dubbed 'occupational pension' households spend, with one person domiciled therein, as much as the 'state pension' household with two residents. The average non-retired household with one inhabitant spends three times as much on leisure goods and services as the state pensioner on his or her own. Motoring costs are illuminating. Their lowness for the state pensioner indicates a paucity of cars at all in that category, as opposed to the huge sums – £51 for

Table 5.11   Weekly household expenditure (in pounds), various categories, showing itemized groups of spending: United Kingdom, 1994–95

	Households					
	Retired				Non-retired	
	State pension		Occupational pension			
	one	two	one	two	one	two
Commodity or service						
Housing (net)	13	21	26	28	42	56
Fuel and power	8	11	11	13	9	13
Food and drink	19	36	24	47	28	55
Essential total	**40**	**68**	**61**	**88**	**79**	**124**
Drink/tobacco	4	9	5	13	15	22
Clothing/footwear	3	6	7	10	11	18
Household goods/services	13	21	28	32	25	46
Personal goods/services	3	6	6	12	6	13
Motoring	2	14	10	38	20	51
Other travel	1	1	2	3	5	8
Leisure goods/services	10	20	24	41	29	62
Non-essential total	**36**	**77**	**82**	**149**	**111**	**220**
Total	**76**	**145**	**143**	**237**	**190**	**344**

Source: Central Statistical Office 1995b

the two-person non-retired home – elsewhere. Indeed, the comparative expenditure on all travel – £3, £12 and £25 for the single households and £15, £41 and £59 for the double households – tells its own story of the mobility differing groups of people enjoy, with all that one may legitimately deduce from that in terms of quality of life. The other facets, such as clothing or household goods and services, are open to similar scrutiny. Most of them might be more lucidly described as ordinary than inessential, for they include so many items – telephone bills, for example, or newspapers – which many would accept as being quite normal, rather than as being the cue to lives of lotus-eating abandon.

What is evident may be poverty, either relative or absolute, and some of that argument was pursued in earlier passages about income. What, more crucially, this portrayal of income presents is an elemental inequality. There are, in turn, arguments to be endured about whether inequality is for good or ill. What is certain is that the average state pensioner is not able to engage him or herself as felicitously with what society has to offer as the average occupational pensioner, let alone the average wage-earner. The average weekly *personal* spending, calculated from these figures, is:

state pension: £74 (which is 56 per cent of what the average occupational pensioner spends and 41 per cent of what the average non-retired person spends);
occupational pensioner: £131 (which is 72 per cent of what the average non-retired person spends);
non-retired person: £181.

Chapter summary

This analysis thus completes its V-shaped attack. From the wide-ranging yearly costs of national revenue for state pensions and the huge expenditure on private pensions, and via the annual income of groups of older people, we have eventually reached the sharp point of the 'V' with an examination of the weekly spending of individual pensioners. In parallel, we have traced the income and expenditure of older people throughout British history, especially through its industrial phase, until the present day; the whole issue rests, ultimately, on that weekly spending of individual old people in the last years of the twentieth century, right down to the specifics of food, fuel, leisure services and household goods.

At this stage, the figures must speak for themselves. Whether the degrees of expenditure are, after the style of Goldilocks' testing of the heat of the bears' porridge, too much, too little or just right, is a matter for personal judgement. And that judgement is always governed, in some regard, by another judgement along the lines of how much society can afford. Of course, those assessments are rarely pure; they are bound in and influenced by the sort of cultural factors mentioned in Chapter 3.

For example, it is ordinarily believed, and putting aside for the moment the question of spending on children, that a retired person does not need as much as a working person, on whose funds travel and perhaps clothing might make particular calls. Yet there is research which suggests that to sustain the same style of life enjoyed in employment as much as 70 per cent of income needs to be retained in retirement (Henle 1972). It is probably not unfair to suggest that the original opinion is influenced by a tacit belief that the retired or unemployed person *should* receive less than the worker as a matter of custom and economic law, and that the supposition that the money is not required follows automatically from that.

There is, of course, as we last noted in Chapter 3, a hidden agenda of income in kind, an array of services to which, personally and collectively, the older person is heir. Health and welfare amenities are the most self-evident – and the most controversial – illustrations of this, but, as it is perhaps a little superfluous to remark, older people continue to benefit from general funding on, for instance, libraries, the police force, refuse collection and so forth. It is to these two aspects – what the older person currently receives in kind and the cultural process through which the public perception is screened of what he or she receives in sum – that we again turn.

Notes

1 The following sections draw strongly on government statistics, critically Governmental Statistical Service (1995) and Central Statistical Office (1995a, 1995b).
2 The following analysis draws largely on Central Statistical Office (1995b). For a fuller elaboration of this form of analysis, see Midwinter (1985).

6

Old age welfare today

Welfare in an ageist climate

When Thomas Jefferson, American founding-father and president, gave up public life, he described himself as enjoying 'senile rest'. He was cheerful and positive in mood, for, in the eighteenth century, senile was a perfectly acceptable demographic term referring to the senior echelon of the population, just like juvenile and infantile. These too have gathered pejorative meanings, but in nothing like the manner in which 'senile' has become a synonym for decrepit or ga-ga. During the nineteenth century ageing came to be seen more and more as a pathological than as a natural process, an interesting medical response to the prevailing social emphasis on strength and power, as betokened by the sports-obsessed 'muscular Christians', colonizing Social Darwinists and money-hungry businessmen of that era. Even now, with ageing more rightfully viewed as an organic process, medical professionals will still refer to 'senile' dementia, where (as the social gerontologist, Alison Norman (1987), has pointed out) were an adult to suffer from a disease associated with childhood, there would be no mention of 'post-juvenile' measles.

Until the depth of such ageism is recognized, it is difficult to comprehend the thinking behind welfare policy ... or perhaps the unthinking. A major problem with ageism is that it is still not generally acknowledged as an insidious and deep-rooted discrimination akin to sexism or racism. Even the most dyed-in-the-wool male chauvinist or xenophobe is at least likely to recognize that others, as feminists or anti-racists, hold contrary opinions. Many people still do not even accept that there is an ageist issue about which to argue. When John Stuart Mill urged the enfranchisement of women at the time of the 1867 Parliamentary Reform Act, he was laughed out of court, even to the point where, at this distance, it is hard to determine whether he was regarded as fool or joker. Ageism is at that stage, when the inferiority of women was scarcely questioned, or, in respect of racism, the pre-1950 period when Caucasian superiority was only just beginning to come under assault – for instance, until the last days of World War II, the American military command forbade the use of rifles by 'negro' troops.

Thus much of the consideration of old age welfare, in cash or kind, is fuelled by this scarcely conscious belief that older people are somehow in decline or are less worthy than younger working people. As we saw in Chapter 3, the cultural determinants of that position during the nineteenth and early twentieth century were extremely strong, and it has only been in the last few years that these have been in any way challenged.

One basic poser is the fact that ageism has come to mean 'old ageism', simply because it has been advocates and agencies involved with older people who have been the first to take up the cudgels. In the interests of intellectual consistency, it must be pressed that age discrimination is wrong across the board. Many who are indignant about men and women being thrown on the scrap-heap (a favourite metaphor) at 60 or 65 and who declare such attachment to birthdays is preposterous, are astounded by the notion that starting school at 5, having a driving licence at 17 or voting at 18 are equally signs of an age-ridden society. The insidious excuse of administrative convenience is urged in defence, just as it was when the civil service pensions were resolved in the 1850s, but birthdays, rather than some test of effectiveness or capacity, has become *de rigueur* in our society. An imaginative, if tiny, illustration is the fairground where the perilous ride does not forbid those under 12 years of age, but which has a mark on the wall by the pay-desk to assess height.

That apologia of practicality was, of course, constantly used to avoid the inclusion of women or ethnic and religious minorities in various aspects of everyday life, and indeed some commentators have proposed that one's age should be legally declared a matter of privacy. It is certainly true that it is difficult to live a week in British society without someone or some form requesting your age (Young and Schuller 1991). A further problem is that some discriminations, not least in older age, are nice rather than nasty. Old age pensioners cope admirably with the humiliation of receiving cut-price or discounted travel, cinema outings or haircuts, little realizing that, were such offers to be made on racial grounds, they might prove to be illegal. During the 1980s there were political moves to grant every pensioner a free television licence. Few commented that this well-meaning notion could be interpreted as divisive and demeaning, and that an increase in the state pension, leaving it to the pensioner to make the independent decision whether or not to invest in a TV licence, was a much less paternalistic approach.

Ageism and old people

Much of this underlines the point made in Chapter 3 that old people believe the propaganda about old age as readily as everyone else, and thus become not only the victims but part of the conspiracy. Again, that is a characteristic which has been apparent in both gender and ethnic considerations. When one is bred in a culture where such beliefs are held to be valid and taken for granted, it is difficult not to share in them. This leads to older people acting out the role of old age, with possible disbenefits such as premature decline. The fitness gap – the chasm which opens up, as one grows older, between what one does and what one can do – is a major example of this (Grimley Evans *et al.* 1993).

The penetration of 'old ageism' into all aspects of social life is worrying. Many voluntary activities, including high-profile public positions and governmental committees, even some of them dedicated to old age, incorporate age limitations on recruitment or termination of service. Jury service, the most long-standing civic responsibility in the Anglo-Saxon canon was until recently flatly halted 'on grounds of age' at 65. Vigorous campaigning had this raised to 70, a step in the right direction, but without a fundamental acceptance that it is the use of birthdays that is wrong. Of course, there are over-70s who may not be well enough to do jury service, just as there may be several under-30s. One has the right of appeal for ill-health and allied reasons. As it is, upwards of seven million people are automatically denied the right to do jury service.

Ageist examples crop up in unlikely places. Advertisers, with a few split seconds to make their televisual pitch, utilize old people quite differently to young people, appealing directly to the stereotypical virtues they know we have absorbed. Hence old women advertise brown bread and soup, rather than shower-gel and deodorant. Design provides vivid instances of the dull, arid, somewhat clinical artefacts often manufactured for older people, despite the promulgation of good practice in some fields. One might quote the difference between the colourful and inventive walking and continence aids for babies and the gray, secretive and grim apparatus given to elderly people. In cinema and on television, older people are used – as in nineteenth-century literature and drama – as the hollow husks, showing the beauty and action of youth in more lucid light. Some standard types – the leering, smutty old man, the ugly 'dame' figure – are retained, even if on occasion attempts have been made to deal more sympathetically with old age, usually by way of wry or whimsical comedy. Every soap opera has its token old residents, usually dispensing homespun philosophies and evoking humorous reaction in equal measure, as faithfully as any Dickensian, Gilbertian or pantomimic oldster.

Invisibility is as great a problem as negativity. In a nation with a fifth of its population in the older bracket, it is their absence from the newspapers and the television screens which is compelling. Whereas people from ethnic minorities are shown on British TV in about the right proportion, and while there is one woman for every two in the population, the representation of older people is only one in three. That is not to blame the televisers and newspeople, any more than the advertisers, for they are only replaying back to watchers and readers their own cultural norms (Midwinter 1991b).

A major element in this process is the very incidence of work. Because the expression of popular culture is so frequently about workers – television series about doctors or lawyers, for example – retired people are shut out from representation. It might be said that retired people have not yet found their consummate and pertinent storytellers – their Dickens or their Mozart – to conjure up for the public the new reality and potential of the third age, just as they have not yet been blessed with the designers and architects – their

William Morris and their Inigo Jones – to do them relevant justice. Interestingly, that engagement with work partially explains why – contrary to the demotic myth – older people are less prone to be the victims of crime than younger people. Indeed, and even allowing for the fact that, not least because of that myth, older people tend to self-apply a curfew and then barricade themselves into their homes at night, according to the British Crime Survey of 1992, people aged 16 to 30 are some six times more likely to suffer crimes against them as old people. The workplace is so often the scene of crime, such as petty theft or minor assault, that retirement acts as a kind of crime prevention.

Talk of law and order reminds that ageist attitudes affect this area of life in curious ways. There tends to be substantial sympathy for the older victim; hence perhaps the excess zeal of the media in reporting such crimes sensationally and without due note of the other variables, such as gender, living alone, type of district. That is understandable enough, but there is also much compassion for the older offender – the elderly, bemused shoplifter, for instance – with a tendency to believe that sickness rather than wickedness, must be the key, and with the official advice of the attorney-general's office militating in favour of non-prosecution and other milder treatments where older offenders are concerned. One recalls Samuel Butler's *Erewhon*, where the sick were punished and the criminals treated as patients.

One could continue, revealing illustrations of latent old ageism in every field, from the age discrimination that afflicts insurance and credit ratings to that which persuades older people to forego many leisure opportunities. Apart from watching television, where older people clock up an amazing 40 hours a week, there is hardly one leisure pursuit on which older people spend more time than their younger brethren. Here is the most grievous paradox of all. Old people, who have been tagged 'the first mass leisure clan' (Dower 1965), have twice as much leisure time as those in the second age of work and parenting, and yet fail to utilize that time constructively. Material barriers, including lack of money, lessened mobility, ill-health and fear of evening travel, play a part, but there are those constant cultural imperatives breeding lack of confidence, suggesting leisure is not so worthy as work, and insisting that old age is a time for social withdrawal and disengagement.

Ironically, the very construct of working and raising a family, by mapping out its own intrinsic timetable, appears to make it easier to plan leisure activity, Retired people, rather like unemployed people, are faced with the quandary of self-discipline, and there may be a tendency to implode or jellify, lured thereby into purposeless lethargy. The Research Institute of Social Change has apostrophized this as 'a trend towards aimlessness, the feeling that life offers little to strive for . . . which is very high among older people' (Midwinter 1993).

Service provision and old age

Yet the ambivalence in Chapter 3 is extremely strong. It is often said that older people are treated as second-class citizens, and this may well be true. Certainly many are excluded through limited funding from several important dimensions of social and cultural life. The corollary is that they are not treated as third-class citizens. That tendency to look after and to look out for older people remains a potent force. It is exemplified at both private and public levels by, respectively, continued family support for older relatives and by a modicum of state provision. During the late 1980s, especially in the United States, there were attempts to whip up intergenerational conflict, along the lines that old people were faring too well in modern societies, to the disadvantage of younger people. There was talk of limiting, even denying, medical attention to people of certain ages (Johnson *et al.* 1989).

It is safe to say that these abrasive and stringent views never took firm hold, precisely because they veered too far away from the equivocal balance, with older people treated with a mix of condescending decency and offhand abruptness. A minute, but pithy, reference might be the residential care officer, who expects to be respectfully spoken to, possibly by official title, but who addresses the older residents, with loud mateyness, by their forenames. Britain treats its oldest inhabitants better than is sometimes thought, but not as well as it might. It gives some money, not a little, but perhaps not enough; the same with services, and all is proffered, if not grudgingly, then resignedly, with a watchful gaze rather than with a liberal spirit. As was noted in Chapter 3, the ageist ambience is difficult to measure, for it amounts to a cultural atmosphere, a miasma drifting over and through society.

What it does is create the psychological parameters within which policy discussions about old age occur. With this all-pervading mist of old age as a comparatively worthless, run-down and passive phase of existence, it becomes that much simpler and more comfortable to ward off demands, say, for extra money or services, so that public opinion remains largely accustomed to and able to live with the ambivalent compromise.

Of course, the essential provision for older people is the same as for the whole of the population. Not only do older people use the same roads, street lamps, refuse collectors, and libraries as the rest of us, they also, particularly in a fiscal regime wedded to retrogressive indirect taxation, pay for such services like the rest of us, through value added tax and allied purchases, as well, in many cases, through direct taxes. It is a question of administrative sensitivity whether or not the service providers consider that, with an ageing population, some of these comprehensive services may require some finer tuning. With some weight in older age, not so much of outright disability, but of a natural growth in hindrances, like failing eyesight or hearing or slowly and weakening of mobility, some care might be additionally required with the smoothness of road paving, the strength and location of street lamps, the method of refuse collection and access to public buildings, such as libraries.

Even in the fields commonly associated in the public mind with old age, the technical and social position indicates a much more cross-generational outcome. As we have seen, poverty is rife in older age, but, equally, there are many well-to-do older people, and there are millions of younger people in poverty. In the mid-1990s a third of social beneficiaries required means-tested supplements to make good the austerity of their flat-rate benefits, many of them pensioners, many of them single parents and others in social distress. Poverty strikes across the board, and it is usual for poverty to haunt the same people throughout their lifespan. Thus most poor old people were previously poor young people, for their working and social existences have been geared in that fashion.

Much of the same is true of other aspects of social life. Residential care is, plainly, of major import for older people. Some 300,000 old people live in some 13,500 residential care homes in the United Kingdom, and that is by far the majority of such residents. But it is not exclusively an elderly enclave. Residential care is provided for children in varied kinds of need, for physically and mentally handicapped people, and for people in other forms of distress, such as drug or alcohol addiction. This chimes in with the story of social welfare, whereby, since medieval times, but substantially during the nine-teenth-century, specialist and inclusive accommodation has been found for social casualties of various kinds.

There are, of course, many intermediary sorts of accommodation, such as sheltered housing, for retired people, but this too is mirrored by smaller scale and independence-oriented provision for children and younger people in social and other difficulties. Were very basic dependency – the ability to get in and out of bed, go to the toilet, and move around fairly freely on one level – the sole yardstick, then only about 200,000 people over 65 would, in fact, qualify, that is, about 2 in every 100 old people. There are several other considerations, notably the proximity of caring support, but one should not exaggerate the degree of call on residential care. Many people are surprised to find that, including the 100,000 older people in nursing home accommodation, only 5 per cent of the elderly population are so catered for, not much more than the 4 per cent which was the 1895 figure 100 years ago. Patently it is not a static population, for the turnover is relatively speedy, and a larger minority of older people obviously move through residential or nursing care at some point of their lives (McGlone and Cronin 1994).

Additionally, and customarily through local authority action under the conditions of the 1991 Community Care legislation, day and domiciliary care is provided to older people, the latest chapter in the continuing tale of services in kind. Help with housework and with meals, and the provision of day centre care, are the most typical examples nowadays of such services, and the whole, including residential care, is subject to a 'ring-fenced' government fund of, in 1993–94, £565 million. It is, perhaps needless to say, regarded by those responsible for the services, such as the Association of Directors of Social Services, to be £250 million short of what is really required, while it must be remembered that many of these amenities are not free but have to be paid for, at least in part, by the recipients. While older people comprise a large bulk of the takers, it must again be stressed that they are not the sole beneficiaries, and that those suffering from physical and mental disabilities may also seek such assistance. It is not retired people as a cohort that are aided, it is self-evidently those old people who are in often dire need. Incidentally, almost a half of non-formal carers are aged 50 to 74, amounting to a fifth of that group, representing some 3.75 million people. In short, a vast proportion of the burden of domestic care undertaken by private individuals, and without which the entire fabric of domestic life in Britain would rapidly come to a halt, falls to the lot of old people. This is in a culture which tends to see old people as the receivers rather than the disposers of voluntary caring (Tinker *et al.* 1993).

Health is another area where there is much soul-searching about the amount of money expended on older people. Sixty per cent of a National Health Service yearly budget of (1993–94 figures) £29 billion was spent on people over the age of retirement, and 50 per cent of the personal social services budget of some £4 billion was utilized in the same cause. One must bear in mind that 'the process of ageing is not an inexorable one determined exclusively by genetic factors, but is greatly influenced by life-style and environment' (Carnegie Inquiry 1993). Nonetheless, there is a necessary decline, even unto death, in old age, and it would be folly to pretend otherwise. Sight and hearing are general examples of that proclivity – over a quarter of those aged 65–74 have a hearing and a fifth have a visual disability. Sixty-six per cent of those registered blind are over 75, just as a half of people over 65 suffer from some form of arthritis and 85 per cent of first strokes occur in that age-group.

One must allow much for perspective. For instance, the incidence of dementia rises from a happily small incidence of 1 per cent in the 60–65 bracket to 30 per cent in the 90+age-group. Many might be surprised to find that 70 per cent of those over 90 were not dementing to some degree. In the wider gamut of mental illness the incidence is much the same across the lifespan. The majority of disabled adults are old, but the majority of old people are not disabled – according to official definition, only 762,000 between the ages of 50 and 79 are disabled. Glasses and hearing aids compensate for many of the sight and sound difficulties.

This is not a complacent attitude; that there will be 800,000 dementia sufferers by the year 2000 is a shocking fact, and one scandalously little regarded. However, ill-health is certainly not an aged preserve. Seventy-eight per cent of retired people report themselves as in very good or in fairly good health, with only 50 per cent finding any health problem at all restricting their activities. Sixty-one per cent of men aged 75+ and 58 per cent aged 65–74 report a long-standing illness, but so do 24 per cent aged 16–44 and 42 per cent aged 45–64. It is right to be mildly cautious of such findings, in that the very ageism of our society might tempt respondents to answer in the context of being in good health 'for my age'. However, it would be unduly prudent not to accept the thesis that ill-health, like poverty, is a structural defect throughout society (Grimley Evans *et al.* 1993). The same is largely true of loneliness, for long the bleak talisman of old age. Much the same percentage of young as of retired people have occasional or frequent intimations of loneliness, with two-thirds of the latter reporting that they have more than sufficient company. Once more, it is not a question of underestimating the problem, but of understanding its manifestations correctly.

It is precisely the belief that older people take more than their fair share of health and allied resources and that they are somehow less worthy than younger people of such help which has led to accusations of age-related rationing and priority schemes. This has been demonstrated in the treatment, for instance, of renal and coronary cases in the United Kingdom. There is some evidence that access to treatment was ruled by age (see Dudley and Burns 1992). Very properly, the bulk of medical opinion takes the view that this is both inappropriate and morally wrong, and that individual assessment and diagnosis should remain the model.

What is surprising in the grudging approach toward old people and medicine is its proponents' unwitting supposition that resource allocation would be more equitable were disease and death to be more smoothly spread across the liferange. The increased survival of human beings, analysed in Chapters 1 and 4, has meant the gradual accumulation of death, and by that token, ill-health, into the older age echelons, and from every viewpoint, that would appear to be a splendid achievement. Ill-health, especially of a virulent nature, is tending to strike later, the consequence of improved nutrition, hygiene, environment, self-care, and it should not of course be forgotten, a higher quality of health care. Even the more pessimistic opinion recognizes, for example, that even if the average length of terminal care required has not been shortened, its occurrence has been postponed. To offer a simplified illustration, a person who half a century ago was needful of a four-year period of hospital or similar attention in his or her 60s, may today require the same amount of treatment in his or her 80s. Most people would judge that a reasonable exchange.

Conversely, other groups are gaining advantages of which older people are largely bereft. Expenditure on education and, to a lesser extent, leisure is extremely high for children and young people, and is well-nigh negligible for old people. This again reflects the assumption that education is almost exclusively child and youth-centred, and that older people have no need for its succour. Advocates of recurrent or lifelong education, the vision of intellectual support at every stage, would beg to differ. With retirements of decades in length, it makes sense to consider the contribution of education and constructive leisure to an enhanced quality of life in that phase.

The whole question hangs on a psychological anxiety about the weight of old age numbers, a worry so pronounced that some commentators have seen within it a half-conscious dread of our own ageing and eventual death. We have noted, in our assessment of the demographic trends, that the demographic horrors have been overplayed, both as they relate to old age of itself and to the general age-profile of the population. For example, it was observed that the joint dependent population, old and young, was much the same as it had been for the last two centuries, and yet policies which suggested shifts of resource from the younger to the older end of the age-range have not been forthcoming.

A constant theme, then, is the usage of oldness as a byword for negative connotations, such as physical deterioration and mental debility. We noted earlier that if an old person is the victim of criminal assault or robbery, it is old age which grips the headlines, as in 'Pensioner Found Battered'. The other variables – gender, size of household, typology of district – may be more significant, but it is oldness which grips the negative imagining. It cannot be said too often that old people are not impoverished or ill or lonely or ill-educated or vulnerable because they are old, but because they are impoverished, ill, lonely, ill-educated or vulnerable.

Privatism and old age

From the standpoint of social policy, it might, for all these reasons, be sensible to respond to the issues of poverty and the other social ills, such as the need for domestic help or ill-health, in a more cross-generational fashion, rather than to treat old age in a separate category. Any scrutiny of the social milieu, as it affects older people, underlines the economic finding that older and penurious people have more in sombre common with younger and penurious people than with older, well-off people. To take two random and non-welfare instances, the married male from the professional classes, living in a prestigious district, has much less to fear by threat of crime than the widow, classified as 'unskilled', residing in an inner-city area; given the current imbalance of car ridership and the vicissitudes of public transport, men in their 70s are twice as mobile, by way of travel, as women in their 50s.

Moreover, the doctrine of privatism has had the effect of exacerbating that tendency. Privatism is not individualism, for it is not so much the operation of a free market as the rigging of a market in favour of those who contribute to and seek advantage from it. Privatism, along with privatization a key dogma of the Conservative administrations since 1979, has already been visited in descriptions in Chapter 5 of private pension schemes. Witness the expenditure of a great public sum, about £13 billion annually in tax relief on the encouragement of private pensions; tax relief on mortgages (of older vintage, it should be said) the popular scheme for the discounted sale of council housing, and the assisted places plan for children to attend private schools at public expense are other examples of the genre. During the 1980s the mortgage relief programme was worth an average of £700 a year to each owner-occupier, a pleasing bonus for, among other mortgagees, people approaching or just into retirement.

Privatism also very much influenced the extension of private residential and nursing care during the 1980s. Social security payment of private fees sprang from £18 million in 1980 to £2 billion in 1993. With decreases in direct public spending, the number of local authority places actually fell from 120,000 to 100,000 in that period, with voluntary agency places remaining at about 25,000, whereas private places jumped threefold from 30,000 to 90,000. As regards private medicine, and apart from the obvious sense in which richer old people are more likely to be able to take advantage of such facilities than poorer old people, there was another example of privatism; tax rebates were offered to those who were prepared to insure elderly relatives for this purpose.

In contrast, there were certain flat-rate benefits available to all pensioners, such as free medical prescriptions and, varying from area to area, discounted or free travel on public transport. However the main force of pension and other policies over the last few years has been to extend the gap between the rich and the poor in older age, taking into account both income in cash and services in kind. It is difficult to avoid the conclusion that money counts, to the extent of seriously infringing the right to equality of opportunity in old age, the opportunity, no less, of enjoying something like an equal share in the good things of life.

We hear much about hypothermia and winter heating, and there are social security payments allowable, in icy circumstances, to help. About one in five of retired people have a problem keeping their house warm in winter; of these about a third blame poor central heating or its absence, the inference being that they cannot afford to solve that problem, while the rest simply plead that they cannot afford to heat their homes efficiently. It is difficult to find a case of a rich

Table 6.1   Comparison of those on low (under £88 per week) and high (over £145 per week) income

Item	All (%)	Low income (%)	High income (%)
Enjoying life more than used to	27	18	38
Good things about growing old – none	29	36	20
Activities; exercise/going for a walk	70	66	80
Find need extra care/attention	50	56	37
No planning of retirement	22	38	4
Often/occasionally lonely	32	45	18
Wish for more social contact	25	33	18
Regular use of car	50	32	74
In receipt of private pension	22	18	42
Sometimes struggle to pay bills	31	53	8
Concern about paying bills	24	39	8
Often/occasionally cut back on basics	28	44	12
Never cut back on basics	72	56	89
No money left after basics paid for	11	19	3
Often/occasional problems with winter warmth	19	30	7
Home with central heating	81	79	90
Council tenancy	24	42	5
Owner-occupation	60	37	87
Married	57	35	73
Single/widowed/divorced	47	65	27

Source: Midwinter 1991a

old person suffering from hypothermia; the question, yet again, is about income rather than age.

A 1991 report extrapolated from its extensive data on retired people over 55 comparative information as between the rich and the poor members of the third age (Table 6.1). It proved to be most revealing, even when presented here, out of its context and in shorthand form (Midwinter 1991a).

First it must be said that with the same data other comparative indicators did not demonstrate the same distinctive characteristics. For example, restriction of mobility, family setting and proximity, and health (73 per cent of those on low incomes reported themselves in very good or fairly good health, against a par score of 78 per cent) do not seem to make manifold differences, although increasing age tends to be correlated with decreasing income to some extent. It must also be mentioned that, even if low income earners are close to the norm on these indicators, high income earners are often far above that mean – for instance, 87 per cent on high incomes report themselves as in very or fairly good health, and only 34 per cent find they have limited mobility – (55 per cent was the norm, with those on low incomes close to it).

Basically, it is only when one turns to a social audit founded on income that major differences appear, bred, as they are, in the everyday comings and goings of ordinary life. Some of the examples are obvious enough: type of tenancy; car usage; the private pension; money troubles. Others are more bothersome. Being single or married makes more of a difference than might have been guessed, whilst the old dance band tune aphorism that 'the best things in life are free' begins to sound flat and distorted. On a whole series of social traits, poorer older people have more difficulty than their wealthier neighbours in adapting to life in older age. They are more likely to be lonely and in need of both extra social contacts and of social care, and they are less likely to be involved in wholesome activities. They just do not seem to get the same excitement or colour out of life, and it is no mystery why, overall, 40 per cent of those on low incomes find life less enjoyable than it was hitherto, and 42 per cent much the same. In one sense that latter figure is more worrying than the former; it underlines the point urged several times in this analysis that oftentimes poor middle-aged people automatically graduate to become impoverished elderly people. It adds up to a picture of rather dismal and grey lifestyles for many of our fellow-citizens, not only in old age but beforehand in the second age.

An interim conclusion

By way of summary, therefore, two or three key pronoucements might be in order. First, it is likely that the ambience of an ageist culture tells against any fundamentally positive reform in terms of approaches to older age. The issues are consistently examined as those of social distress, with older people in need viewed as social casualties; when old age matters are under review, the Department of Health nationally and the social service departments locally tend to take the lead, a clear indication that, officially and popularly, oldness and illness are practically synonymous. It is, it should be emphasized, a benign and not a hostile attitude; the universal and time-honoured precept of 'ambivalence' reigns supreme. However, there can be little doubt that, until and unless decision-makers and opinion-formers, and the public at large, reconstruct their psychological image of what old age now is or could be, there is small likelihood of anything more than a tinkering and a tampering with the status quo in respect of old age.

Second, those many members of the retired population who are on short commons financially, who might be defined as being chiefly reliant on state pensions and public services for their upkeep, suffer a double jeopardy. Because of the strong functional power of income as an index of quality of life, they are victimized on the one hand by dint of being old and retired people, subject to scant and often condescending provision, and on the other in contrast to their wealthier fellows in the same age-echelon. The combined effects of owner-occupation, of possible savings and inheritance proceeds, and of solid occupational pensions, against a deterioration in direct state funding and service levels, has dramatically contrived to stretch the gap between rich and poor in old age. Furthermore, an emphasis on regressive indirect taxation at the expense of progressive direct taxation – an apt illustration might be the relative difficulty faced by the two groups in response to the value added tax on fuel and power in recent years – and the inroads of privatism conferring additional advantages to the already well-off, merely serve to underscore that position.

Third, pains have been taken in this study to relate older people, where relevant, to their fellow-citizens in the younger age-groups, and it has been constantly urged that almost all the disbenefits which beleaguer poor and needy old people are structurally the same ones which disadvantage poor and needy people of all ages. By that token, it should be quickly added, the benefits which accrue to the better-off in old age are precisely the ones which, given the construct of modern Britain, featherbed the well-to-do of all ages.

It follows that, if one is seeking a more cohesive and less divisive collectivity of older people in the twenty-first century, then one is faced with two interchangeable and extremely daunting tasks. One is to rid the nation of the scourge of ageism, and the other is to secure something closer to socioeconomic equity, not only in older age, but throughout the entirety of society. The final chapter will attempt to address both those somewhat mind-boggling issues.

PART III

Future perfect? Post-work people tomorrow

7

Older age in the twenty-first century: The real

The necessary and the likely

Lady Blanche, addressing the female students of Castle Adamant in the Gilbert and Sullivan comic opera *Princess Ida*, considers the Is, the Might Be and 'the inevitable Must'. Speculation about the future, in regard of everything from retirement and pension policy to Derby winners, may range from the Utopian dream of the 'Might Be' to the dystopian nightmare of the 'Mighty Must'. Just as you could possibly back the outsider which romps home at 100 to 1, it is probably more likely that you'll lose your shirt on the flawed favourite. So is it with retirement and pensions, and there the gamut from the optimistic to the pessimistic may possibly be encompassed by what is necessary and what is likely. One might argue, with a decent mix of rationality and sentiment, for the kind of policy which would be equitable and, in the sense of bringing about social cohesion, necessary, or one might discern, from the political record of the recent past, the kind of policy which, while failing to promote equity, would probably amount to the dismal, but not fatal, outcome of more of the same.

Moving for metaphorical aid from the seedy world of the race-track to the lofty reaches of political philosophy, the two classical lines of descent in that discipline are usually deemed to stem from the real of Aristotle and the ideal of Plato, from, pragmatically, the best practical result to, ethically, the best moral consequence. This section is mapped along much the same lines, albeit in more humdrum key. It attempts to provide an account of what the runes foretell if no fundamental shift in thinking and initiative occurs, and what might be achieved were such a basic change of belief to happen.

It is, at bottom, about political philosophy. It is about dwelling and bargaining in an everyday world of moral men and women, themselves caught up in the organic processes of history and geography, and without too much

Table 7.1 Older people in the European Union

Nation	Population		Life expectancy at 60		National income per capita (ECUs)	%GNP All	Social expenditure		% Social expenditure on			Social expenditure per capita (ECUs)	% 65+ in households		Labour force %			65+ poverty Nat. index 100
	%>19	%<55	Male	Female			pensions	health	old	health	unemploy-ment		1 person	3+ persons	Agri-cultural	Industrial	Service	
Belgium	25	26	18	22	10,600	35	12	6	44	34	13	3400	32	29	3	31	66	181
Denmark	24	25	18	22	15,000	34	9	5	38	31	13	4700	38	5	6	27	67	253
France	28	25	18	22	12,500	34	12	6	45	34	7	4000	33	20	7	30	63	136
Germany	21	27	18	22	13,500	26	12	6	42	41	7	4200	39	18	4	41	55	141
Greece*	20	12	18	21	4,300	20	11	4	not known			720	15	35	27	25	48	153
Ireland	37	19	16	20	6,800	26	6	7	31	34	16	1700	20	30	16	29	55	76
Italy	24	26	18	23	9,700	26	12	5	59	33	2	2700	25	36	10	32	58	129
Luxemburg	23	25	17	22	12,800	33	21	5	44	44	1	4000	23	28	4	29	67	144
Netherlands	26	22	18	23	11,400	31	11	7	42	46	11	3800	31	12	5	27	68	91
Portugal	29	24	18	22	2,700	15	7	4	42	46	3	636	18	45	21	35	44	139
Spain	29	24	19	23	5,600	15	7	4	46	35	17	1200	14	30	14	32	53	125
UK	26	26	17	22	10,500	21	7	5	43	31	8	2700	30	11	2	33	65	119

Note: *The Greek figures are >14 and <65.
Source: chiefly derived from Crosby 1993

connection with abstraction. In that mundane circumstance, the two conflict-
ing positions are not extreme or out of reach. The more pessimistic scenario
points to a system which trundles on, ensuring that most, perhaps all, older
people would be rescued from the direst impoverishment, and many would
exist at a reasonable level. It would not be calamitous, but, for many tastes, too
few of those older people would be enabled to live really pleasant and
productive lives, and there would be too wide a rift for social comfort between
rich and poor people. The more optimistic blueprint suggests a position in
which all older people would be sufficiently funded to live enhanced lives of
dignity and civic value, and in circumstances of greater social alliance and
equality. It is, from what the tarot cards of social guesswork currently reveal,
improbable, but it is crucial to urge that it is not impossible or impractical. It is
achievable.

The European perspective[1]

It is now customary to place an analysis such as this in its international,
typically its European, context. That wider view offers some evidence as to
whether the United Kingdom lags behind or leaps ahead of normal standards
in comparable countries, as they affect the lifestyle of older people. A glance
across, therefore, offers a suitable chance to look ahead. Especially in the
shorter term, ideas might be spotted which could be adopted with advantage,
while changes might be argued on the grounds of European parity.

The comparative findings are perhaps best presented in tabular form, with
the ultimate alphabetical placement conveniently falling to the United
Kingdom, thereby making for easier checking (Table 7.1). The figures are
adapted from data from the late 1980s in all cases, and they have been freely
rounded up, in part for simplicity of comparison, but also in part because of the
nature of the information. Obviously, the social, political and economic
character of the 12 nations reviewed varies considerably, so that each figure
might represent a mesh of different aspects. It was deemed safer to opt for
rounded figures to underline the insistence that they should be used as
indicators rather than as fully-fledged and incontrovertible conclusions.

Some further comments may be necessary. The under-19 and over-55
proportions of the national populations were chosen as the clearest index of a
number of allied points. It has been suggested, in the British context, that 55+
is a wiser marker of the third age, in terms of the end of work and of mainline
parenting, than 60 or 65; hence that cut-off point was picked for all the
countries. Then again, it was strongly argued that the relationship of the two
cohorts of dependants, the younger as well as the older, needed to be
acknowledged, that the overall social responsibility of the second age (or
working and parenting population) might be sensibly considered. Nineteen
and under was selected, rather than, say, 16 and under, as allowing something
for higher education and something for youth training schemes and unemployment. Apart from the 'young' profile of Ireland, the remarkable trait is
the close similarity of the figures, with seven nations, the United Kingdom
included, having the two echelons within three percentage points of each
other.

Most of the figures are alike, with Britain not at all abnormal in this respect, and this applies even more so to the figures of life expectancy at 60 for males and females. The similarities are indeed amazing. Europe is ageing, if not gracefully, then equitably. The indicator of wealth, based on national income per capita and transcribed into the all-embracing ECU, tells a different tale, one of greater riches at the core of the European Community and greater poverty at its fringes, specifically, Greece, Ireland, Portugal and Spain. From the purely nationalist viewpoint, the United Kingdom, with 10,500 ECUs per head, stands close to the mean of, approximately, 9,600 ECUs, just as it stands midway in that particular listing which has Denmark at the top with 15,000 ECUs. Britain remains a moderately rich nation, even by western standards.

One might have expected that national wealth would have dictated some of the spending patterns on social expenditure, and the figures for Spain and Portugal uphold the hypothesis. However, the UK is low in the European league of social spending, with but 21 per cent of its GNP devoted to such causes, compared, for example, with Belgium's 35 per cent. In fact, the United Kingdom is ninth in the division, and that has an obvious knock-on effect in respect of pensions (all pensions are covered by these figures, but 'old age' predominates to near-exclusivity) and health care (much of which, but of course by no means all, is expended on older people). Expenditure on health is nearer the norm than that on pensions, but the comparison with Belgium or the Netherlands, countries with similar wealth profiles and not too remote culturally, is not very edifying from a British standpoint.

The same raft of statistics were next seen from the angle of their percentage of the actual expenditure on social welfare in each member-state. Ireland appears to be a little on the miserly side, whereas Italy is, according to taste, either extravagant or generous. Otherwise, the UK is at much of a muchness with its continental partners, and the range of health expenditure, which so affects the life quality of older people, shows another narrow gamut from most to least costly, although Britain looks a trifle too prudent on that scale. Unemployment costs vary more wildly, probably reflecting more the number of unemployed in particular countries than undue differences in their treatment. Then it is back to the realities of national wealth with social expenditure expressed in ECUs per head of population. Despite recent increases, Portugal and Greece, and to a lesser extent Ireland and Spain, do not fare too well as compared with the heavier expense of Denmark, France and the Benelux countries. Britain maintains that typical half-way house position with 2,700 ECUs; the mean for that scale of figures is 2,800 ECUs.

The two household figures form, to some degree, a mirror-image. The more industrialized and richer nations tend to have more older people living alone (Germany, 39 per cent, for instance) than the more agricultural and poorer ones (Greece, 15 per cent) – and vice versa apropos extended families. Households, including older people, which have three or more people resident, veer from the 5 per cent of Denmark to the 45 per cent of Portugal. Britain (30 per cent alone; 11 per cent three or more) tends toward the former side, as one might expect. The three-generational household is a rarity in Germany and Denmark (2 per cent of the total), but is still 12 per cent in Portugal and Greece. The British figure of households, that is, those which have a youngster under

15 and, ordinarily, a grandparent over 65, is but 4 per cent, the same as in Belgium and the Netherlands.

This begins to paint a picture of the provision of care, for, as we noted in earlier chapters, the balance of domestic and institutional care alters according to factors like the agricultural or industrial nature of the economy and the attendant amount of urbanization. It should be recalled that 'domestic' and 'institutional' should not be used pejoratively; living alone may be about independence and dignity; living in an extended family may be about unpleasantness and hardship.

The triple configuration of the labour force throws light on the same kind of issue. Agriculture, essentially another industry in the most developed economies, requires no more than 3 per cent in Belgium or 2 per cent in Britain for personnel purposes, whereas Portugal and Greece still have a much larger slice of their labour force engaged in such agrarian activity. What is perhaps of most interest, especially in terms of future possibilities, is the huge proportion of European employment which is neither industrial nor agricultural, but service. Two-thirds of the workforce of several of the core European nation-states are in this very modern category of men and women providing services of all types. These indices of wealth, accommodation and labour participation are of value in making more careful and detailed comparisons, and in judging whether the United Kingdom is in front of or behind its neighbours in regard to older age and the relevant policies. It enables one approximately to compare like with like.

The poverty index, the final scale on the chart, is defined as having a disposable income which is less than 50 per cent of national average equivalent expenditure, with the national poverty rate set at 100. The table shows that most EU nations fail to protect their older citizens from 'average' poverty; on these findings, something like 8.5 million EU citizens over the age of 65 are suffering poverty. Ireland – a recent major improvement – and the Netherlands appear to be efficient in the defence of their older subjects against poverty, with Denmark lapsing badly. It is stressed that these numbers are based on internal standards; some of Denmark's poverty might be quite luxurious in Greece.

Sometimes replacement ratios are utilized to demonstrate the worth of pensions. This is a snapshot of the average manual worker's wage and a full initial pension, which for instance shows French pensions delivering about three-quarters of a reasonably healthy wage of 14,000 ECUs. Again, the internal differences must be watched. Portugal replaces the average wage with a pension of 82 per cent, but the base – 5000 ECUs – is very low, while Dutch pensions have a low replacement value of about a half, but the wage is high – some 18,000 ECUs – and as we just noticed, the Netherlands has a good record of avoiding old age poverty in a well-to-do economy. The United Kingdom fares none too attractively on this measure, for its pension involves only a 33 per cent replacement value of a wage rated at 16,000 ECUs.

These are complicated comparisons. Measured against many of the yard-sticks, Britain tends to occupy a midway place in any resultant league table, which on the face of it is not too critical. The worrying feature is that Britain seems, by that token, to fall a little behind the nations which are immediately comparable. It seems often to be the least of the better, that is, the richer and more developed nations such as Denmark, Germany, Belgium and the Netherlands. Although there has, of late, been a substantial move toward uniformity in the European treatment of older people – for instance, the use of 65 for pension eligibility is the norm in many countries, with the United Kingdom in the process of shifting to that age for its female pensioners – there continue to be differences of indexation, supplementary and occupational extras and the like. Thus the process of comparison is not simple.

Casting the net a little wider, the British methodology has enjoyed much in common with that used in Japan, Canada and Sweden as well as EU countries like Denmark and the Netherlands. This involves a flat-rate pension, a means-tested 'income support' type safety-net, and a linked and often compulsory earnings related scheme. However, the British programme varies in that the basic eligibility is by contributions rather than, as in some other countries, straightforward age and domicile; while there is, of course, much opting out from the earnings related element. In the USA, as well as in Belgium, Germany and France, the emphasis is more on the earnings related component, plus the usual safety-net. The old-time social insurance principle, associated with Bismarck, still rules. Australia now has a means-tested state pension and obligatory occupational pensions, whilst the Netherlands, with its high initial state pension, does not insist on an earnings related addition. It is of significance that, where universalism by rate and by eligibility reigns, women, who in general have not in the past enjoyed the same employment opportunities as men, are advantaged. This is not the case in Britain, where women are often reliant on their husband's contributory pattern or zeal in saving for an occupational pension.

Overall, however, it is hard to dodge the assessment that, were the United Kingdom to employ the same criteria of its associate countries which are nearest in character, it would probably result in a genuine increase in pension provision, whether by basic or supplementary means. In general terms, as of 1991, the UK was spending a little less than the European average – 43 per cent as opposed to 45 per cent of all social benefits – on older people. This was in conditions where slightly more of its population was in the third age (26 per cent over 55, one of the EU's four highest) but as regards economic activity, with 81 per cent men (58 per cent women) aged 55–59 and 55 per cent men (20 per cent women) aged 60–64 still working, as against respectively 72 per cent of men (35 per cent of women) and 36 per cent of men (14 per cent of women) in Europe at large. There is, as ever, another gloss on this; some foreign economists and politicians would congratulate their British counterparts for so successfully bridling in the state expenditure on these items and transferring so much of the action into the private sector, to wit, the pension funds.

It may not be, all in all, a major discrepancy, except that the United Kingdom has an economic inheritance of nineteenth-century grandeur and a post-war reputation of giving the world a lead in health and welfare legislation. There is little doubt that European relativities, even when all the variables have been considered, suggest that the UK has some catching up to do. The question remains as to whether the catching up will amount to low-scale refurbishment – the likely – or major reform – the necessary (Crosby 1993).

The background to the likely

Currently the problem is couched in terms of changed circumstances rather than philosophic belief. The system which worked well enough from the late 1940s through to the early 1970s has come unstuck. Full employment and economic growth furnished the means to fund a welfare mechanism of reasonable standards. Now mass unemployment and economic uncertainties have returned to render this largesse a tricky proposition, precisely at a moment when, through earlier retirement and greater survival into older age, the demand for such support extends.

A preliminary point must be that, in mourning the passing of Beveridge-inspired welfarism, we should not, as is our wont in the composition of the obituary, extol its virtues too charitably. It was – it never claimed to be more – a scheme of social protection against temporary social set-backs, with retirement, not foolishly for the time, seen almost as temporary as a period of sickness or unemployment. That is, it was conceived as a comparatively short phase after a full working life. What it achieved on the whole was the extinction of absolute poverty, in the sense that thereafter the construction of the modern welfare state, there was little or no starvation or extreme want. Even then, there were a few loopholes, of which death from hypothermia through an inability to pay fuel bills is but one example. In general terms, however, the conquest of absolute poverty was achieved, and this was a notable success, against the much less comprehensive schemes which had preceded the 1940s settlement. At the same time, we should not forget to nod in appreciation of the brilliant public relations coup of the originators of the old age pension all those years before. By using the general post office, rather than the poor law authorities, for its dissemination, they removed much of the stigma attached to public provision in old age, even if they did not much improve its substance.

On the other hand, neither the original old age pension nor its updated Beveridge version made but minor inroads into the problem of relative poverty, roughly defined as the exclusion of people as a result of insufficient income, from the normal social intercourse and activity of the ordinary citizen. Especially during the 1960s, this rediscovery of poverty was particularly marked. It was noted that the lifestyle of poorer and richer old people was eventually so different as to make it socially difficult to consider them as members of the same group. What must be realized is that a return to the good old days of the 1950s would be the revisitation of a consciously unequal society, and not the gladsome rush back to an old age El Dorado.

Nonetheless there is much gloom about the future. The original Beveridge plan to link benefits to contributions actuarially, and build up a strictly determined reserve fund on this insurance principle, was swiftly overtaken, as we noted early in Chapter 5. This arose because of the generous impulse to give pensioners wholesome financial life, the relatively small number and tiny benefit period of the recipients, and unexpectedly rapid economic growth. By

1958 insurance funding had become pay-as-you-go funding, in effect a form of direct taxation by way of contributions. Its saving grace was that it was bespoke taxation, in that the effort was made to ensure a balance of income and expenditure year on year, while the overt nature of the transaction did sustain the notion of a contract between the generations, with workers paying into a treasure trove from which they would ultimately take advantage.

The weight of the fund drew the attention of those who saw in welfare legislation a slide toward dependency on the 'nanny state' and an inhibition on personal initiative, a critique which burgeoned in the late 1970s and the 1980s. One gloss on this was the suggestion that the guarantee of a state income in older age was an impediment to personal savings during the working life, with a consequent ill-effect on the national regime of borrowing and investment. It has to be said that whereas private pension funds play a very full role in such matters, the public pension funds do not – although theoretically they might – in that they are preoccupied with financing immediate payments. That said, these theories rest on somewhat indeterminate and implausible ideas about the behaviour of income-earners, and the all-round effect of social security pensions on savings may be small.

A greater perceived difficulty is the switch in the favourable demographic balance of the generational contract. The danger with non-insurance funding is that its two-phase process – contributing worker/benefiting pensioner – does not occur in a socioeconomic vacuum but in a world subject to swings and vacillations. The chief illustration of this is the existence of a second age of workers, hammered by unemployment and vocational transience, subscribing to the upkeep of a third age, larger in number and lengthier in survival. The dwindling value of the British state pension has already been mentioned, and it is, in major part, a consequence of this anxiety.

It is true that the reduction in the numbers in the first age to which we have constantly referred, must be entered into the equation. The public expenditure on children is, unsurprisingly, lower than that on older people. It is estimated that over the next 50 years, whilst there will be reductions in the main OECD countries of a fifth in education expenditure and something less than a fifth in family benefits, health costs will grow by two-fifths and pension costs by four-fifths. It has been calculated that, because of these population changes, social expenditure bills may rise by a third over this period (OECD 1988a). It must be stressed that these figures relate to public costs, bearing in mind that the majority of older people across the developed nations rely almost entirely on state grants for their income. Children and young people do not. They are financed, privately, that is out of the income of their parents, and it is not easy to enter those variable and intangible costs into this equation.

Nonetheless, income not so expended might be utilized elsewhere, in savings, for example, and so the roller-coaster of the debate continues. A striking point, for instance, made by several commentators, is that the huge investment of the private and occupational pension funds is so predicated on large and quick returns, often from overseas markets, that it is damagingly short-term apropos the solid and longer-term needs of the British economy. Such savings on this analysis have by default severely disrupted the structural base of business and industry in the United Kingdom and the honest employment of its workforce. It is a discussion which is taking place not in a static but in an organic, even a volatile, set of conditions.

That proviso must be accepted when looking at some approximate findings about the increased share of national income spent on pensions resulting from demographic shifts, assuming similar benefit patterns and employment levels of today. In the United Kingdom, the figure of 7.5 per cent of national income deployed on pensions, which is confidently forecast for 2000, would by 2040 have risen to 11 per cent. Elsewhere the leap would be higher: from 16 to 31 per cent in Germany; from 8 to 15 per cent in the USA; from 13 to 29 per cent in the Netherlands. The OECD average is expected to be 11 per cent in 2000; 20 per cent in 2040. That is almost a doubling, whereas the British estimate suggests but a half increase, and from a lower base. Whether that is a matter for solace or for anger is a personal-cum-political response; the average British worker pays out £13 a day on social security, but, where some might see that as alarmingly high, others might view it as alarmingly inadequate.

In terms of the responsibility placed on the working population over that same period, and calling the 1980 base 100, the figure for 2000 would be 96 and for 2040 it would be 111. Comparable rates for other countries would be: Germany: 113/154; USA: 96/131; and the Netherlands: 104/139. These are admittedly crude calculations, but they indicate a growth in the so-called burden of social expenditure (that is, not only pensions), although as we consistently discover, the British ratio of 96/111 suggests, for better or for worse, that the United Kingdom is a little behind the norm for like nation-states.

One economic element which tends to be overlooked is productivity. The setting of worker against pensioner forgets why worker became pensioner. It was the productive capacity of the economy, betokened by the advance of technological science, which allowed, even forced, men and women to retire, and in general terms, radically reduced the quantum of work needful of being performed. During the later years of the 'golden age' of full employment and economic growth, the demographic factor, whilst already meaningful, accounted for only a quarter of the increase in social welfare costs in the developed nations. The other three-quarters were down to more generous provision and wider eligibilities, such as reduced pensionable ages. It was, then, more a response to the economic change than to the demographic change. That outcome – a wholesale mix of economic pressures and political reactions – is almost certain to remain the key (OECD 1988b).

The most likely

In the mid-1990s that compound of economic and political elements continues to point in much the same direction as before. A plethora of proposals has been ushered forth for public contemplation, from political parties and policy institutes and from specially formed commissions of enquiry and academic groups. Although the details vary substantially, a consensus does appear to be emerging around a two-tier guarantee of income in older age. The two components would be an ongoing, relatively small state pension and an assurance that each person would have some form of top-up pension related to means.

It is a proposition which owes most to past and little to forward thinking. It brands the older person at once with a double stamp: that of social casualty and that of ex-worker. On the one hand it argues that there should be the absolute satety-net of the flat-rate state pension, although, true to the tradition of the poor law and the old age pension, the safety-net would not be held very far above the hard floor of impoverishment. It is constantly urged that even the restoration of the state pension to its original earnings-related level would be over-costly. The price-related indexation of the pension has reduced it in value, as we have seen, to as little as 15 per cent of average male wages (1995 statistics) and to boost it to the 1979 earnings-related valuation of about 20 per cent of gross male earnings, nearly £7 billion would be required immediately, an increase rising to £50 billion in 2030.

On the other hand, the proposition claims that personal savings over the workspan should be deployed more comprehensively, with occupational pensions very much the model. Various proposals have been made about how this might be achieved. These are offered in the sombre shadow of a private pensions industry which has been heavily criticized for incompetence and worse, with the scandals, flaring in the early 1990s, around the pension arrangements associated with the tycoon, Robert Maxwell, serving as the most vivid testimony. They have also been proposed in the dark shade of a SERPS scheme for state occupational pensions, agreed with ostensibly cross-party support in 1975, which was shattered barely 11 years later under the fears of heightened public expense, and in which just 17 per cent of employees remain. Whatever else, these shifts in both the private and the public arena remind us that it is a swiftly moving process; one generation can never be sure what the coming generation will or can provide, or the previous generation demand by way of care and expenditure.

Most of these putative schemes personalize the process. Whatever degree of direct state control or indirect state regulation is intended, the idea of saving a pot of gold out of earnings over the working life is at the base of almost all of them. In the main, it would be an ordered, indeed obligatory, course of action, very much more 'insurance' than 'pay-as-you-go' in style. The state would, according to particular versions of these plans, either manage these investments or ensure that the agencies existed which would manage them. The outcome would be a pension related directly to one's income and to its reasonable replacement, with 50 per cent often cited; the precedents are numerous in the occupational pension field.

The progenitors of such programmes have to face two types of interim case. These relate to people who are already retired or close to retirement, and who have little or no extra resource of this kind or opportunity to engage with such a scheme; and closely linked with them, those who, through sickness, misfortune, unemployment or inadequately paid work, are not in a position to benefit from income-oriented provision. The answer lies in some form of – vogue word – 'targeting'. This typically means attempting to meet the requirements of the most needy by extra funding, which always sounds suspiciously like our old friend, the additional payment, previously seen in its guise as an extra allowance during the poor law days or as a supplementary benefit of some kind later on. It might entail maintaining instalments on a pension plan during periods of unemployment, or supplementing the flat-rate pension for those who have not been able to provide themselves with adequate cover.

One fairly liberal version of these several plans aims to guarantee everyone an income equivalent to the old-style earnings-related pension through the mechanism of the 'assured pension'. This would be accomplished by a relatively small basic pension plus a means-tested second-phase pension for those who needed it; that is, those whose occupational or private pension left such a shortfall. In addition, there would be a second tier compulsory alternative to occupational pensions, paid for out of employer/employee contributions, alongside a phasing out of SERPS. Interestingly, because both the government and the private funding bodies are to some degree suspect in this respect, there are now calls, as with the assured pension/second tier top-up scheme, for an independent but carefully regulated body – the Funded National Pension Scheme – to manage these proposals, that is, an agency free from both the vagaries of politics and the avariciousness of commerce (Anson 1996).

Of course, all of these plans may be interpreted generously or meanly, but their fundamentals are recognizably the same. They would sustain a lowish subsistence form of universal pension (although some right-wing thinkers have toyed with its rank abolition) together with an all-embracing system of occupation/income-based personal pensions, with some intermediary supports for those not catered for by this device.

Work remains the determinant. The well-paid, regular worker ends up with a good income in older age; the ill-paid, irregular worker doesn't; the former edges towards the 'ex-worker' pole and the latter slides towards the 'social casualty' pole. Although more organized and all-encompassing, it establishes no basic change from the past. Where there is change, it is of degree rather than of kind. It relates to the surging overlap of the two types of pension. In the past, it was unusual to have two pensions, a state benefit and an occupational payment. Increasingly it will be more usual to have dual provision. Almost everyone might retire with the universal and with an occupational pension of some kind.

That does mark a cultural change from the origins of the modern welfare state. It indicates a shift in public thinking from the collective to the personal. The mood of the Beveridge era, forged in the blazing fires of World War II and its aftermath, had something about it of the spirit of the Three Musketeers; 'all for one, and one for all'. The National Health Service, paid for by all and free to all at the point of delivery, was the most ambitious and the most popular instance of this mood, and it is one which has endured nobly. More recently, the public temper has been more inclined to privatism, and independence has been aligned with the taking of personal responsibility. Instead of paying taxes for everyone, one makes personal investments for oneself and one's family.

The affluence of the period after 1950 left its mark. One must not be too disingenuous about that fledgling affection for the welfare state. Readers must be reminded that the majority of voters then did not pay taxes, and were perhaps more cheerfully prepared to vote for politicians who insisted that the well-to-do minority should pay more taxes. By the end of the 1940s a married man with two children did not pay income tax until his earnings were over 100 per cent of average earnings: today he would be paying tax before they had reached 33 per cent of the average. So there are distinctive grounds for voters being a little more chary than of yore when collective solutions are mooted.

At the same time, it would be foolish to presume that the self-centred and solo timbre of the national psyche is any more likely to last than the choral unison of the post-war commonwealth. Neither is nor has been exclusive, and some commentators argue, sometimes possibly a trifle wistfully, that the collective music has been soft, not silent. One of several variables or wild cards which should not be discounted is a cultural mood-swing to a greater sense of commonalty. Some of the same discussion might be applied to that other aspect of provision, services in kind, previously considered in Chapters 3 and 6. Were the public climate to change significantly, in terms of how it felt about both cash and services in kind for older people, possibly within an atmosphere in which older age came to be viewed much more positively and colourfully; were that to happen, then something closer to the ideal might be accomplished. To that discussion we now repair in the last chapter.

Note

1 Crosby (1993) is the source for most of the material here cited.

8

Older age in the twenty-first century: The ideal

Citizenship and cohesion

Moving by way of conclusion from what is likely to happen to what might happen for the best, it is perhaps apposite to begin with a consideration of what is wrong with the former, the 'real', solution. It is not so much in the detail, which, according to which variant of which scheme is envisaged, ranges from rather good to rather bad, as in the very basis of that solution that one might find fault. To put it bluntly and squarely, the state plus top-up sort of pension scheme is too oriented toward work, in a situation where the salience of work has declined.

When retirement was ordinarily less focused, shorter and more piecemeal, it might have made some sense to use work experience as the chief determinant of post-work income, along the lines of an occupational pension. It might almost have been described as a longish holiday with pay, at the end of, rather than during, working life. What the schemes with a work-related element – which, in practice, is all of them – fail to take sufficiently into account is the reduction of work as a sheer quantity of time in the lives of men and women. Throughout this study, we have witnessed the dwindling proportion of work as a part of how people spend their time.

Compared with our own society in the past, and compared with most other societies in the past, the amount of time actually spent working has, for the majority, decreased from being central to marginal over the lifespan. An aspect of this has been the lengthening of the retirement phase. To the extent that the third age may be regarded as a discrete stage in the lifecycle, the question must be raised as how we wish people to disport themselves in this new and largely unprecedented position. If, as is often urged, we aspire for older people to contribute as active and well-motivated citizens, realizing their best selves individually and granting socially productive benefits to the community, then the subsequent question must be, how do we fund them to do that? In other words, the debate must, in all political propriety, assume a civic character as well as an economic one. It is about the political bottom line being not subsistence, but participation. It is about joining in rather than getting by.

For some there may be a moral overtone. For those who regard social cohesion as a respectable social and political goal, there may appear to come a point where the gulf between the least and the most well-endowed financially produces the opposite effect; that is, a socially divisive community. Because one touchstone of social cohesion might arguably be the capacity of all citizens to involve themselves, comfortably and positively, in the normal comings and goings of everyday society, it follows that the funds to enable this to happen must be adequate. More than that, the inference might also be drawn that, if some have substantially more income than the majority, then social cohesion may be distorted and warped from the top as well as from the bottom of the social pile.

This is not a plea to examine exact, mathematical equality of income. One recalls the economist whose solution to society's economic problems was to collect all the money together and then divide it up equally among all citizens. The corollary was that, when he had spent all his share the money should be collected again, and redistributed. That old chestnut demonstrates the difficulties of precise equality in a sophisticated economy. However, for a practical exercise in egalitarianism, it is distinctly possible to construct parameters, high and low, within which incomes might decently rise and fall. One rule of thumb suggested is that, in any workplace or unit of employment, the most senior salary should not be more than four times the size of the most junior wage. This would allow, among other considerations, for reasonable, but not excessive, differentials for responsibility, experience and qualification.

During the mid-1990s there was much discussion about a minimum wage. If that were, as mooted in 1995, about £4 per hour, and assuming a 40-hour week, a minimum weekly wage of £160 would result. Two points arise from that. One is that it is already a far cry from the single weekly pension, and, from the viewpoint of citizenship and in recollection of the analysis in Chapter 5 of what constituted reasonableness of income, there might be a forceful argument that the basic pension and the minimum wage should be in close relationship. The other is that, for all the chatter about a minimum wage, there has been a deathly hush on the topic of a maximum wage. Now an open-ended policy on income at the top level soon incommodes any essay at social cohesion, for the very highly paid are, in social terms, soon outbidding their fellow-countrymen and women, to such an extent that social communion and intercourse with them would prove arduous, even impossible.

For example, it would be hard to make the case for a society where an old age pensioner (or, of course, an unemployed person) has an income of less than £100 a week, remaining long in a state of social well-being and coherence, where the highest income is more than, say, £1000 a week. Looked at in the round, apropos what in humdrum terms might be seen as the normal and current fruits of the good life, it is difficult to make the case for anyone earning more than, at an approximate venture, £100,000 per annum, which is near enough £2000 a week. It must be stressed that this is not a statistically-based calculation; it is an attempt to raise a social poser as plainly as possible, with the assistance of some educated guesses about income levels.

It is at this point that an issue, mentioned in passing, is forcibly entered into the discussion; namely, the matter of differentials relating to skills and responsibilities. This involves the general influence of market forces on incomes, and the fashion in which, most notably, the prosperous entre-preneur, the adulated pop star or the gifted sports-person earns teeming millions. Market forces, of course, do not operate as abstractions or as a consequence of spontaneous combustion. Human beings have actually to spot and respond to such influences with decisions of one kind and another. During the early 1990s there was some angst expressed over the senior executives of British public interest utilities who granted themselves great salary increases and other monetary awards, their claim being that, in so doing, they were obeying the strict commands of the market.

It is not a simple subject, but some research has shown that the effects of incentives such as this, or conversely of punitive taxation, on high-flying earners in business and elsewhere has been overstated. A lay opinion might be that those who cry loudest in support of such a regime are those who most benefit. The comedian Jimmy Edwards, in one of his shows in the 1950s, standing as a 'Jimunist' mock-parliamentary candidate, used to rant: 'There is no housing shortage; the housing shortage is merely a rumour spread about by those who have nowhere to live'. Similarly, the necessity for high-income theory may be a rumour spread about by those who enjoy one. In practice, it is difficult to believe that completely efficient people could not be found to perform most functions at more rational salary levels. Indeed the pious thought occurs that they might perform them more efficiently in that their motives would be less selfishly inclined.

Early in 1996, the American economist, Professor Frank, speaking at Cornell University, claimed that the standard salaries of chief executives in the USA were now 120 times the pay of the average worker, whereas they had been only 35 times that average in the 1970s. In that relatively short period, albeit the one during which unemployment and insecure employment had become more of the norm, the top 1 per cent of the workforce had captured 70 per cent of the growth in earnings. The USA in particular, and developed nations in general, now formed, he added, a 'winner take all' society. Moreover, his researches suggested that flat-rate taxation, highly favourable to big salary earners, did not stimulate growth but encouraged 'more wasteful competition for the top slots . . . the wannabes in these contests, if they were diverted into more traditional career paths, would produce things of great value' (Frank 1996).

Be that as it may, even if astronomical differentials were required to maintain the stability of the economy and other systems, it does not follow that they are needed in the third age. Indeed, there might even be an argument for restarting and rescheduling life in acknowledgement of the discrete status of the third age. One might envisage some rough and ready 'equality of opportunity' operating, rather like the liberal view that, in the first age, there should be 'equality of opportunity' operating for children, principally in educational chances. Wryly, the impediment to the full implementation of that credo has been, in part, the existing wide differentials in income in our society. Research has consistently shown that, on balance, children from well-to-do homes fare better than their poorer schoolfellows; the same has also been shown to be true of the hoped-for equality of access to the health and welfare services. The 1967 Plowden Report (DES 1967) and the 1980 Black Report (DHSS 1980) were, respectively, but two examples from a huge literature demonstrating the heavy weighting of the socioeconomic determinants.

What this means is that youngsters in the case of the education services, and everyone in the case of the health services, arrive at the starting-line of equal opportunity with widely varying personal wherewithal. They are more or less well-equipped individually to take up the cudgels of opportunity, and therefore it becomes more a uniformity than an equality of opportunity. Much of this qualitative difference stems from financial support. George Bernard Shaw justly said that it might not matter if, because of income, a docker did not socialize with the Astronomer Royal, but it was wrong that the same inequality made it impossible for their children to do so.

The massive inequality of income in old age means that this sort of factor, widely recognized in the educational field, is deliberately built in, so that, faced with the opportunities offered by older age, some are generously advantaged financially, while others are gravely handicapped. In day by day practice, what might be the fortuitous accident of becoming, in adolescence, a shop assistant or a civil servant, crucially determines one's quality of life aged 85 or 90, perhaps 25 or 30 years after retirement. So much hangs on the happenstance of whether one finds oneself in the vocational groove which provides a good salary and a good pension.

The scales of social justice begin to creak a little. Some might contend that these are just rewards, the prizes for selfless endeavour and lofty achievement. Life, parodied in this regard, comes to resemble a series of preparations for jam tomorrow: childhood is spent preparing, through examinations and the like, for the working arena; working life is spent, through occupational pension contributions and savings, preparing for retirement. In any event, that moral case might be turned on its head. It might be pressed that the prizes do not always relate to talent or conscientiousness or the communal value of the tasks undertaken. All kinds of dualisms might be proffered by way of illustration; the diligent shop assistant versus the indolent civil servant; the shifty entrepreneur versus the devoted nurse. At this juncture, the neo-realists are inclined to fall back on some form of atavistic argument, that these are laws of nature, that this is how life is, that this is the luck of the draw. However, we exist in a socioeconomic environment which is largely man-made, and thus changeable by men and women. There is not much natural about it. The only fundamental question is whether the men and women in our particular society would be prepared to accept such basic revisionism.

The reader's eyebrow might have been raised over this lurch into the overall field of income policy for everyone. But we must eventually return to initial statements made in this study that poverty and riches in old age are not functions of old age in itself, but derive almost entirely from the character of the economy as a whole. It is only possible to solve the problem of poverty in older age by solving the problem of poverty at all ages, for the first is normatively the product of or a subgroup of the second. One speaks here of the erasure of relative poverty, rather than absolute poverty, in the sense that no one would be so richer or poorer than his or her neighbour as to mar the aim of social compatibility. In the context of this immediate discussion, that would entail something like a regime which incorporated a minimum or basic income for all at a relatively high level, along with a progressive tax system reaching almost total claw-back at a comparatively low level (see for example Parker 1984).

It would certainly have to involve something like a return to the Beveridge prerequisite of full employment – but full employment would have to be redefined yet again. There would need to be a lively elasticity of the labour market. We have seen full employment defined in Victorian times as working long hours, with scarcely any holiday or break, from immature youth to ripe old age. We have then seen, in the second half of the twentieth century, full employment made manifest with a much later start and a much earlier finish, with much shorter hours and a generous holiday leave allowance. In future, that flexibility will have to stretch still further, so that full employment may enjoy a new vogue in the age of new technology. This would require, for instance, and according to the typology of job and other factors, a compound of job-sharing, structured part-time working, four-day weeks, three-week months, the month off a year, the taking off of a sabbatical year, and other such devices. The aim would be to share the employment as equably as the income, with both subject to a copper-bottomed guarantee in pursuit of a society based on fairness and a social contract of give and take.

The price of citizenship and cohesion

Something of that radical kind would be essential as the canvas against which to promote the notion of greater equity of income in older age. It is, needless to say, a question of political persuasion and judgement. Some may find in the current inequality, albeit with its reasonable safeguards against total social disaster, the nearest to some version of an ideal, perhaps laying emphasis on a social framework acting as stage for the playing out of personal initiative, ambition and adventure.

What is difficult to gainsay is the radical nature of the change that would be involved, were it to be agreed that older people should be treated more equally and more generously. However it is important to reflect on the political, as opposed to the economic, nature of the change. Faced with large-scale increases in public spending, it is customary to defend the status quo with the cant remark that the nation cannot afford such expenditure. That is not strictly true, or, at least, it is only half the truth. Given that Britain is still a rich country by international standards, the truth is rather that the nation cannot afford such expenditure, unless it is prepared to make wholesale changes in the way it deploys its gross national product. Almost the total case against a huge increase in income maintenance for older people is encapsulated in the overworked phrase about what is 'politically realistic'. The initial task perhaps is to change the pigmentation of political realism.

Although it would be foolish to believe, as some occasionally do, that the road to higher pensions for all is straight and smooth, it would also be silly to pretend that the journey could not be undertaken. It is a route which is more unimaginable than unattainable.

Building on the analysis presented in Chapter 5 about income and expenditure rates in older age, it was calculated by the author in 1995 that 'the suggested personal cost for what passes as active membership of modern British society' was £125 a week, or £6500 a year. At much the same time, a modest but adequate budget of £121.08 a week for a pensioner or £204.49 for a pensioner couple was cited. The £125 suggestion comprised the following items, reflective of the pattern used in that chapter:

Housing	£ 40
Fuel and power	£ 10
Food	£ 20
Clothing/footwear	£ 5
Household goods/services	£ 15
Transport	£ 15
Personal/leisure services	£ 20
Total	£125

If a minimum income of £125 was accepted as the ideal solution, it would be, to utilize some Euro-jargon, a demogrant. That is it would be paid to everyone, without fear or favour, by dint of residence in the nation and whatever criterion of eligibility – entry into the third age, for instance, at the end of paid work – was agreed. Importantly, such a demogrant would be for everyone, and the outdated Victorianism of the married couples' depleted pension could be banished. In the broader term, it might come to represent the accepted basic minimum income for everyone, young or old. As a matter of essential political presentation, it might be valuable also to abandon the terminology of the pension, and refer to this as a 'social wage'. It would be the salary paid to every older person to be an active and productive citizen.

The first step would be to engineer a situation where all older people were, from public or private sources, guaranteed this minimum social wage, before moving to a position where we simply paid older people this decent income for the sheer pleasure of their company and for their social product in the here and now, irrespective of what has happened or what they have done in the past. Gradually, work might cease to be the crucial dictator of post-work income. The basic pension would advance to meet the common need, and the occupational pension would retreat to the same end. Those in the second age would produce the wherewithal for the first age, in appreciation of having passed safely and, one hopes, happily through it, and for the third age, in pleasant expectation of a fulfilling experience yet to come.

It would, needless to say, be expensive, but in the longer term, it would be legitimate to consider not only what is provided by the state now, but what is funded by the pension companies, for, in that the state-based wage might come to be regarded as the central income, the need for a work-related additional pension would decline. Through taxation, either direct or hypothecated, as through the equivalent of National Insurance contributions, the workforce would be paying now to live later. Bear in mind that this would be in an atmosphere of relative equality, where the gap between incomes, either in older age or in society at large, would be narrower, with, for instance, a cap on third age income, given a minimum of £125 of, say, £500 per week, or £25,000 a year (Midwinter 1995).

The day this was written it was announced that Cedric Brown, who had been chief executive of British Gas for 15 months, was retiring aged 61, with a consultancy fee of £120,000 a year and a pension £246,000 a year, a sum of £366,000. Although one could fund some 6310 single state pensions from that astronomical amount, it would be naive to think that what used to be called squeezing the rich would make possible a reasonable income for the 10 or 11 million people in the third age. Certainly, fairer shares would ease the economic pressure on tax and National Insurance payers or their future equivalents. Nonetheless, the fundamental question is whether, as a society, we truly believe that it contributes to social stability and cohesion when one pensioner retires on an income of over 6000 times the income of another.

The current economic position is not, of course, confined to the United Kingdom; rather it is part of a global process, with the abundant pressures of international trading and multinational commercial activity. The effect of the United States of America and of other key players in this economic game is critical, and, admittedly, it would be difficult for one country, such as Britain, to undertake unilateral reform of its socioeconomic circumstances. In these connections, it is interesting to recall the Cornell University economist, Professor Frank and his comment about 'wasteful competition for the top slots' with their corresponding large financial rewards. Without the fixation on high salaries, attention can be given to other, arguably more valuable, things.

This again underlines the reasons why the argument is a civic, social and political one, rather than just an economic one. That is why this study has laid such an emphasis on the image of old age and the way this affects the provision, not only of income, but of services to older people. If the citizenry of the country could be persuaded of the legitimacy of the argument for a social wage in an egalitarian context, then the plumbers and carpenters of the Treasury and other fiscal agencies could apply their undoubted technical skills to the business of working out the most effective *modus operandi* and the one with the least disbenefits to the economy at large.

The call for a socially cohesive community is not new. During the famous 1647 Putney debates, associated with the Levellers at the end of the English Civil Wars, Vice-Admiral Thomas Rainborowe claimed, 'for really I think that the poorest he that is in England hath a life to live as the greatest he' (Midwinter 1985).

In conclusion

Meanwhile, back at the ranch of 'the politically realistic', the likelihood is that the perceived economic, and not the idealized civic, version of income and retirement policy will carry the day. Work, however its impact on the body politic dwindles in terms of quantitative personal engagement, will probably continue to rule the day, and the referential frame of widely varying income differentials will persist. Relative poverty in older age, as in the younger age cohorts, will, in spite of the well-intentioned but minor repairs of the pension policymakers, remain. Economic travails will ensure that active participation in the civic and social life of the community will be impeded for many older people, and they will be handicapped from joining others of their peer-group on anything like equal terms.

Let us review the situation from the standpoint of the mid-1990s. At present, all employees and their employers, whose pay exceeds the Lower Earnings Limit, fixed at about the level of the state pension itself, pay National Insurance Contributions. These are on a sliding scale, which is open-ended for the employer and close-ended, at about seven times the Lower Earnings Limit, for the employee. There are separate arrangements for the self-employed. These contributions are expected to make up the National Insurance Fund to a point sufficient to meet the ongoing requirements of the pension scheme, with the annual receipts being some £45 billion including interest on investment.

Although now somewhat bedraggled, the SERPS scheme is paid for out of the National Insurance Fund, but those who contract out of SERPS, by dint of belonging to another occupational or private plan approved by the authorities, receive a rebate. For instance, in 1994–95 such rebates cost the Fund well over £7 billion. Income support for older people, the present manifestation of the age-old safety-net, is paid for out of general taxation, along with other social security benefits.

As for occupational pensions, these are either predicated on defined benefits, where the employer must underwrite the scheme while the employee sticks to a static contribution, or on defined contributions, where the benefits may vary according to the success or otherwise of the investment. Private pension arrangements are reliant on the contributions of employee and employer, but many are based solely on the rebated monies available from the National Insurance Fund.

As of 1995–96, the basic pension is £58.85 for a single recipient and £94.10 for a married couple. This is now slightly less than Income Support, which is £65.10, single, and £101.05, for a couple. The official, if slightly dubious, configuration claims that a couple require but 160 per cent of a single income to arrive at the same standard of living. To recapitulate further, 10 million people are in receipt of this basic pension, but the gender difference is significant. Almost every man of pensionable age, that is, over 65, receives the basic pension, but, in respect of their own contributions, less than a third of women are in similar benefit. Regulations introduced in 1978 have begun to alter this position. It was only in that year that 'home responsibilities protection' was introduced to cover the contributions of (mainly) women needing to care for a child or sick person, while, until 1978, many married women had taken advantage of the chance to opt out of their contributions. Less than half of married women receive any basic pension in their own right, and it will be well into the next century before all will receive some, albeit in many cases a smallish proportion, of that basic pension.

It will be remembered that many pensioners – about three million – are in receipt of means-tested benefits, to the tune of £7.5 billion, made up of Income

Support and housing and council tax benefit. That is in addition to the £27 billion needed to sustain the basic pension. Another £2 billion is spent on SERPS, although, at present, the four million takers do not receive very large sums. It was, of course, the fear of voluminous expansion of SERPS which caused the scattering of its contributors to the occupational and private market, with such an effect that only 17 per cent of employees remain in the scheme, the majority of them both women and on relatively low salaries. Two-thirds of employees are, conversely, contracted out of SERPS, the great majority of them being members of occupational pension programmes, leaving only about 15 per cent of employees without any second-tier cover above the basic flat-rate pension. It should be added that there are additional personal tax allowances for the over-65s, with over three million pensioners seizing this advantage to a cost to the state of about £1 billion in a full year.

In toto, and including sickness, disability and widows' benefits, the sum expended on older people by the state was estimated, in Chapter 5, at £38 billion for 1994–95. This is delivered fairly equitably across the income range, although, if anything, the middle and upper tiers tend to benefit more, partially the result of a full work pattern of contributions leading to a full pension. Distributed according to total income, the bottom decile of pensioners receives £92, the top decile £113, and the middle two deciles approximately £140 a week from the state. The differences are chiefly concerned with what is drawn from occupational and private pensions and savings; those on the lower incomes obtain almost all their income from the state; the rest have substantial extras. The top decile enjoys an income (1992–93 figures) nearly six times as great as the bottom decile, that is, roughly £550 to £90 per week, although, needless to say, those averages mask a considerable taper at both ends (Anson 1996).

That is the present picture. For all its modernistic jargon and twentieth-century frame, it looks extremely like the Victorian picture apropos the balance of public and private monies involved, the condition of services in kind, and the ageist climate in which the whole process is negotiated. The portents strongly favour an extension of the entire mechanics, doubtless with a new patois to describe the detail, beyond the millenium. How far we remain away from the aspiration of the great English Ethical Socialist, R.H. Tawney, who believed that society should provide the resources which would enable everybody 'to grow to their full stature, to do their duty as they see it, and – since liberty should not be too austere – to have a fling when they feel like it' (Tawney 1952). For too many older people, the current and anticipated arrangements for retirement income mean that they will make do – but they will not make merry.

Selected further reading list

Age Concern England (1994) *The Pensions Debate: A Report on Income and Pensions in Retirement*. London: Age Concern England.

Anson, Sir J. (chairman) (1996) *Pensions: 2000 and Beyond*, Report of the Retirement Income Inquiry, vol. 1. London: The Retirement Income Inquiry.

Atkinson, A. (1994) *State Pensions for Today and Tomorrow*. London: King's College.

Atkinson, A.B. and Sutherland, H. (1992) Two nations in early retirement? The case of Britain, in Atkinson, A.B. and Rein, M. (eds) *Age, Work and Social Security*. Basingstoke: Macmillan.

Barclay, Sir P. (chairman) (1995) *Joseph Rowntree Foundation Inquiry into Income and Wealth*, a summary of evidence prepared by J. Hills, vols 1 and 2. York: Joseph Rowntree Foundation.

Barr, N. and Coulter, F. (1990) Social security: Solution or problem? in Hills, J. (ed.) *The State of Welfare: The Welfare State in Britain since 1974*. Oxford: Oxford University Press.

Bosanquet, N., Laing, W. and Propper, C. (1990) *Elderly Consumers in Britain: Europe's Poor Relations?* London: Laing and Buisson.

Bradshaw, J. and Lynes, T. (1993) *Household Budgets and Living Standards*. York: Joseph Rowntree Foundation.

Bury, M. and Macnicol, J. (eds) (1990) *Aspects of Ageing: Essays on Social Policy and Old Age*. London: Royal Holloway and Bedford New College.

The Carnegie Inquiry into the Third Age Final Report (1993) *Life, Work and Livelihood in the Third Age*. Dunfermline: The Carnegie United Kingdom Trust.

Commission of the European Communities (1993) *Older People in Europe: Social and Economic Policies*, The 1993 Report of the European Observatory. Brussels: EC.

Commission on Social Justice (1995) *Social Justice: Strategies for National Renewal*, The Report of the Committee on Social Justice. London: IPPR.

Dahrendorf, R., Field, F., Hayman, C., Hutcheson, I., Hutton, W., Marquand, D., Sentance, A. and Wrigglesworth, I. (1995) *Wealth Creation and Social Cohesion in a Free Society*. London: Committee on Wealth Creation and Social Cohesion.

Davies, B. (1994) *Better Pensions for All*. London: IPPR.

Department of Social Security (1994) *Security, Quality, Choice: The Future for Pensions*, Cmnd 2594. London: HMSO.

Dilnot, A., Disney, R., Johnson, P. and Whitehouse, E. (1994) *Pensions Policy in the UK: An Economic Analysis*. London: Institute for Fiscal Studies.

Field, F. (1995) *Making Welfare Work: Reconstructing Welfare for the New Millenium*. London: Institute of Community Studies.

Goode, R. (chairman) (1993) *Pension Law Reform*, Report of the Pension Law Reform Committee, vols 1 and 2. London: HMSO.

Hancock, R. and Weir, P. (1994) *More Ways Than Means: A Guide to Pensioners' Incomes in Great Britain During the 1980s*. London: Age Concern Institute of Gerontology.

Hills, J. (1990) *The State of Welfare: The Welfare State in Britain Since 1974*. Oxford: Oxford University Press.

Jefferys, M. (ed.) (1989) *Growing Old in the Twentieth Century*. London: Routledge.

Johnson, P., Dilnot, A., Disney, R. and Whitehouse, E. (1992) *Incomes: Earnings and Savings in the Third Age*. Dunfermline: The Carnegie United Kingdom Trust.

Johnson, P. and Falkingham, J. (1992) *Ageing and Economic Welfare*. London: Sage Publications.

Laczko, F. and Phillipson, C. (1991) *Changing Work and Retirement*. Milton Keynes: Open University Press.

National Association of Pension Funds (NAPF) (1994) *Securing the Future*. London: NAPF.

Organization for Economic Cooperation and Development (OECD) (1988a) *Ageing Populations: The Social Policy Implications*. Paris: OECD.

Organization for Economic Cooperation and Development (OECD) (1988b) *The Future of Social Security*. Paris: OECD.

Organization for Economic Cooperation and Development (OECD) (1988c) *Reforming Public Pensions*. Paris: OECD.

Smeaton, D. and Hancock, R. (1995) *Pensioners' Expenditure: An Assessment of Changes in Living Conditions 1979–1991*. London: Age Concern Institute of Gerontology.

Social Security Advisory Committee (1994) *State Benefits and Private Pensions*. London: HMSO.

Taverne, D. (1995) *The Pension Time-Bomb in Europe*. London: Federal Trust for Education and Research.

Townsend, P. and Walker, A. (1995) *The Future of Pensions: Revitalising National Insurance*, Discussion Paper 22. London: The Fabian Society.

Whiteford, P. and Kennedy, S. (1995) *Incomes and Living Standards of Older People*, Discussion Paper 34. London: DSS.

World Bank (1994) *Averting the Old Age Crisis: Policies to Protect the Old and Promote Growth*. Oxford: Oxford University Press.

References

Ackroyd, P. (1990) *Dickens*. London: Sinclair-Stevenson.

Anson, Sir J. (chairman) (1996) *Pensions: 2000 and Beyond*, Report of the Retirement Income Inquiry, vol. 1. Folkestone: Shelwing.

Barker, P. (ed.) (1984) *Founders of the Welfare State*. London: Heinemann.

Beveridge, Sir W. (1942) *Social Insurance and Allied Services*, The Beveridge Report, London: HMSO.

Bowman, M.J. and Anderson, C.A. (1963) Concerning the role of education in development, in Geertz, G. (ed.) *Old Societies and New States*. London: Macmillan.

Burgess, E.W. (1962) in Kaplan, J. and Aldridge, G.J. (eds) *Social Welfare of the Ageing*. New York: International Association of Gerontology.

The Carnegie Inquiry into the Third Age Final Report (1993) *Life, Work and Livelihood in the Third Age*. Dunfermline: The Carnegie United Kingdom Trust.

Central Statistical Office (CSO) (1991) *Social Trends 21*. London: HMSO.

Central Statistical Office (CSO) (1995a) *Annual Abstract of Statistics*. London: HMSO.

Central Statistical Office (CSO) (1995b) *Family Spending: A Report on 1994/95*, Family Expenditure Survey. London: HMSO.

Cipolla, C.M. (1962) *The Economic History of World Population*. London: Penguin.

Collins, D. (1965) The introduction of old age pensions in Great Britain. *The Historical Journal*, 8(ii): 246–56.

Covey, H.C. (1988) Historical terminology used to represent older people. *The Gerontologist*, 28(3): 291–7.

Covey, H.C. (1989) Old age portrayed by the ages-of-life models from the middle ages to the 16th century. *The Gerontologist*, 29(5): 692–8.

Crosby, G. (1993) *The European Directory of Old Age*. London: Centre for Policy on Ageing.

Crowther, M.A. (1978) The later years of the workhouse, 1890–1929, in Thane, P. (ed.) *The Origins of British Social Policy*. London: Croom Helm.

Department of Education and Science (DES) (1967) *The Plowden Report: Children and their Primary Schools*. London: HMSO.

Department of Health and Social Security (DHSS) (1980) *Inequalities in Health: Report of a Research Working Group*. London: DHSS.

Dower, M. (1965) *Fourth Wave: The Challenge of Leisure*. London: Civic Trust.

Dudley, N.J. and Burns, E. (1992) The influence of age on policies for admission and thrombolysis in coronary units in the UK. *Age and Ageing*, 21(2): 95–8.

Elton, G.R. (1953) *The Tudor Revolution in Government*. Cambridge: CUP.

Falkingham, J. and Gordon, C. (1990) Fifty years on: The income and household composition of the elderly in London and Britain, in Bytheway, B. and Johnson, J. (eds) *Welfare and the Ageing Experience*. London: Avebury.

Fiegehen, G. (1986) Income after retirement. *Social Trends*, London: Central Statistical Office, HMSO.

Finer, H. (1994) *The Theory and Practice of Modern Government*, 4th edn. London: Greenwood.

Finer, S.E. (1952) The Life and Times of Sir Edwin Chadwick. London: Methuen.

Frank, Professor (1996) Quoted in *The Guardian*, 10 February 1996.

Government Statistical Service (1995) *Social Security Statistics 1995*. London: HMSO.

Graebner, W. (1980) *The History of Retirement: The Meaning and Function of an American Institution 1885–1978*. New Haven, CT: Yale University Press.

Great Britain (1895) *Report of the Royal Commission on the Aged Poor*, Eyre and Spottiswoode for the HMSO, London.

Grimley Evans, J. (1993) *Can We Prolong Our Lives? The CIBA Foundation Debate*. British Association for the Advancement of Science. Keele: University of Keele.

Grimley Evans, J., Hodkinson, M., Goldacre, M., Savory, M. and Lamb, S. (1993) *Health and Function in the Third Age*. Oxford: Nuffield Provincial Hospitals Trust.

Hancock, R. and Weir, P. (1994) *More Ways Than Means: A Guide to Pensioners' Incomes in Great Britain During the 1980s*. London: Age Concern Institute of Gerontology.

Henle, P. (1972) Recent trends in retirement benefits related to earnings. *Monthly Labour Review*, 95(6).

Hobsbawm, E. (1994) *Age of Extremes: The Short Twentieth Century 1914–1991*. London: Michael Joseph.

Hutton, W. (1994) *The State We're In*. London: Jonathan Cape.

Johnson, S. (1775) *Dictionary of the English Language*.

Johnson, P., Conrad, C. and Thomson, D. (eds) (1989) *Workers versus Pensioners: Intergenerational Justice in an Ageing World*. Manchester: Manchester University Press.

Johnson, P. and Falkingham, J. (1992) *Ageing and Economic Welfare*. London: Sage Publications.

Keane, J. (1995) *Tom Paine: A Political Life*. London: Bloomsbury.

Laslett, P. (1984) The significance of the past in the study of ageing. *Ageing and Society*, 4(4): 379–89.

Laslett, P. (1989) *A Fresh Map of Life: The Emergence of the Third Age*. London: Weidenfeld and Nicolson.

Lowe, R. (1993) *The Welfare State in Britain Since 1945*. London: Macmillan.

McGlone, F. and Cronin, N. (1994) *A Crisis in Care? The Future of Family and State Care for Older People in the European Union*. London: Family Policy Studies Centre.

Midwinter, E. (1985) *The Wage of Retirement: The Case for a New Pensions Policy*. Policy Studies in Ageing No. 4. London: Centre for Policy on Ageing.

Midwinter, E. (1986) W.S. Gilbert: Victorian entertainer. *New Theatre Quarterly*, 3(11): 273–279.

Midwinter, E. (1990) An ageing world: The equivocal response. *Ageing and Society*, 10: 221–8.

Midwinter, E. (1991a) *Attitudes to Ageing*. London: The British Gas Report.

Midwinter, E. (1991b) *Out of Focus: old age, the press and broadcasting*. London: Centre for Policy on Ageing.

Midwinter, E. (1993) *Citizenship: From Ageism to Participation*. The Carnegie Inquiry into the Third Age. Dunfermline: The Carnegie United Kingdom Trust.

Midwinter, E. (1994) *The Development of Social Welfare in Britain*. Buckingham: Open University Press.

Midwinter, E. (1995) *Raising the Wage of Retirement*. London: Age Concern England.

Minois, G. (1989) *A History of Old Age: From Antiquity to the Renaissance*. (translated by S.H. Tenison). Oxford: Oxford University Press.

Norman, A. (1987) *Aspects of Ageism*. London: Centre for Policy on Ageing.

Northcote, S. and Trevelyan, C. (1855) *Report relative to the reorganisation of the civil service* 268 (1870) House of Commons, London.

Office of Population and Census Studies (OPCS) (1992) *General Household Survey*, Government Statistical Survey. London: HMSO.

Office of Population and Census Studies (OPCS) (1996) *General Household Survey 1994*, no. 25. London: HMSO.

Organization for Economic Cooperation and Development (OECD) (1988a) *Ageing Populations: The Social Policy Implications*. Paris: OECD.

Organization for Economic Cooperation and Development (OECD) (1988b) *Reforming Public Pensions*. Paris: OECD.

Parker, H.V. (1984) *Action on Welfare*. London: Social Affairs Unit.

Phillipson, C. (1982) *Capitalism and the Construction of Old Age*. London: Macmillan.

Playfair, L. (1845) *Second Report on Large Towns and Populous Districts*. Parliamentary Papers xviii, House of Commons, London.

Raphael, M. (1964) *Pensions and Public Servants: A Study of the Origins of the British System*. Paris: Mouton.

Read, D. (1979) *England 1868–1914: An Age of Urban Democracy*. London: Longman.

Roberts, D. (1960) *The Victorian Origins of the Welfare State*. New York: Yale University Press.

Royal Commission on the Aged Poor (1895) Parliamentary Papers XIV, February.

Savage, S.P., Atkinson, R. and Robins, L. (eds) (1994) *Public Policy in Britain*. New York: St Martin's Press.

Sims, George R. (1903) *The Dagonet and Other Poems*.

Smeaton, D. and Hancock, R. (1995) *Pensioners' Expenditure: an assessment of changes in living standards 1979–1991*. London: Age Concern Institute of Gerontology.

Tawney, R.H. (1952) *Equality*, 4th Edn. London: George Allen and Unwin.

Thane, P. (1978) The muddled history of retiring at 60 and 65. *New Society*, 45(826): 234–6.

Thane, P. (1982) *The Foundations of the Welfare State*. London: Longman.

Thomas, K. (1977) Age and authority in early modern Britain. *Proceedings of the British Academy*, 107(62) London: Oxford University Press.

Thomson, D. (1984) The decline of social welfare: Falling state support for the elderly since early Victorian times. *Ageing and Society*, 4(4): 451–82.

Thompson, C. and West, P. (1984) The public appeal of sheltered housing. *Ageing and Society*, 4(3): 305–26.

Tinker, A., Askham, J., Grundy, E. with the assistance of Hancock, R., McCreadie, C., Whyley, C. and Wright, F. (1993) *Caring: The Importance of Third Age Carers*. The Carnegie Inquiry into the Third Age. Dunfermline: The Carnegie United Kingdom Trust.

Trinder, C., Hulme, G. and McCarthy, U. (1992) *Employment: The Role of Work in the Third Age*. The Carnegie Inquiry into the Third Age, Dunfermline: The Carnegie United Kingdom Trust.

Tylecote, A. (1992) *The Long Wave in the World Economy*. London: Routledge.

United Nations (1986) *World Population Prospects*. New York: United Nations.

Walters, P.B. (1981) Educational change and national economic development. *Harvard Education Review*, 51(1).

Weber, M. (1983) *On Capitalism, Bureaucracy and Religion*. (edited by S. Andreski) London: George Allen and Unwin.

Young, M. and Schuller, T. (1991) *Life After Work: The Arrival of the Ageless Society*. London: HarperCollins.

Index

References in italic indicate figures or tables.